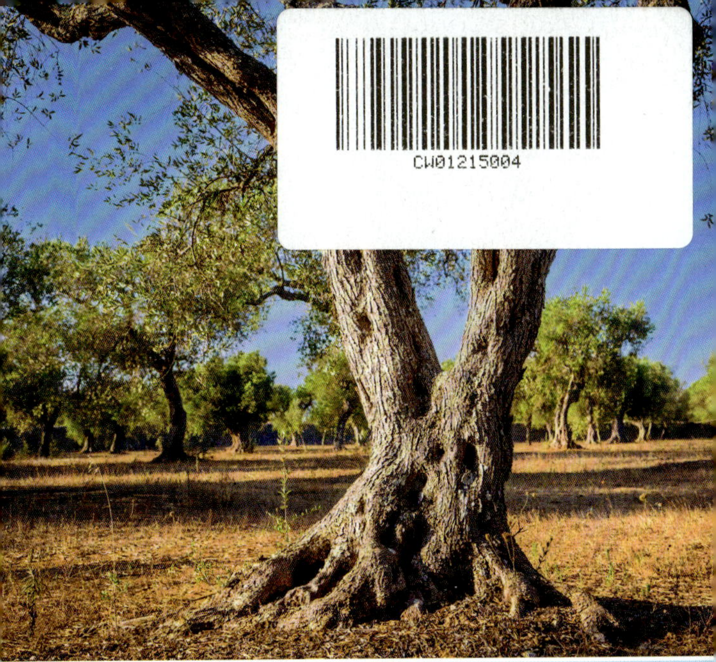

THE MINI ROUGH GUIDE TO
PUGLIA

Tailor-made trips and unique adventures crafted by local experts

Rough Guides has been inspiring travellers for more than 35 years. Leave it to our local experts to create your perfect itinerary and book it at local rates.

Don't follow the crowd – find your own path.

HOW ROUGHGUIDES.COM/TRIPS WORKS

STEP 1 Pick your dream destination, tell us what you want and submit an enquiry.

STEP 2 Fill in a short form to tell your local expert about your dream trip and preferences.

STEP 3 Our local expert will craft your tailor-made itinerary. You'll be able to tweak and refine it until you're completely satisfied.

STEP 4 Book online with ease, pack your bags and enjoy the trip! Our local expert will be on hand 24/7 while you're on the road.

PLAN AND BOOK YOUR TRIP AT
ROUGHGUIDES.COM/TRIPS

HOW TO DOWNLOAD YOUR FREE EBOOK

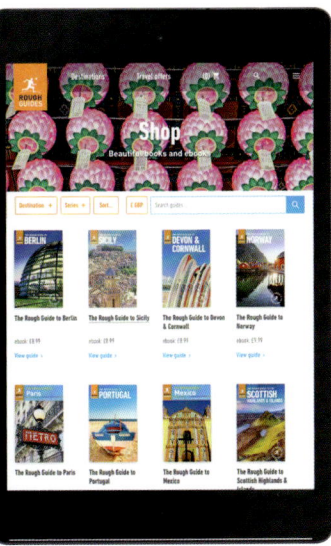

1. Visit **www.roughguides.com/free-ebook** or scan the **QR code** below

2. Enter the code **puglia916**

3. Follow the simple step-by-step instructions

For troubleshooting contact: mail@roughguides.com

10 THINGS NOT TO MISS

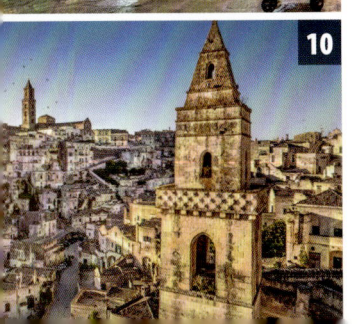

1. **GARGANO PENINSULA**
   Ravishingly beautiful spur with stunning coastline and an ancient forest for hiking and biking. See page 27.

2. **TREMITI ISLANDS**
   Glorious archipelago of tiny islands, surrounded by glittering turquoise seas. See page 33.

3. **CASTEL DEL MONTE**
   A unique medieval masterpiece reflecting the humanism of its founder, Frederick II of Swabia. See page 38.

4. **TRANI**
   Elegant coastal town with a dramatically sited Romanesque cathedral and a finely restored historic centre and port. See page 42.

5. **ALBEROBELLO**
   The centre of Puglia's famous *trulli*, the quaint, conical-roofed houses. See page 53.

6. **MARTINA FRANCA**
   Large and lively town, known for its finely-preserved Baroque monuments and gastronomy. See page 55.

7. **LECCE**
   Puglia's Baroque gem, packed with lavish architecture and fanciful facades. See page 63.

8. **OTRANTO**
   Historic port with a picturesque old quarter, stunning cathedral and good beaches nearby. See page 70.

9. **GALLIPOLI**
   Charming historic town with fishing harbour and good seafood restaurants. See page 74.

10. **MATERA (IN BASILICATA)**
    Fascinating troglodyte town of ancient grottoes and rock-hewn churches. See page 80.

A PERFECT TOUR

Day 1

Vieste. Make the Gargano Peninsula your base for three nights (it's a long haul from Brindisi or Bari airports). Stay at the seaside resort of Vieste, surrounded by coves, cliffs and excellent beaches. But avoid July and August. Stroll through the historic centre, feast on fish creations at Capriccio, then chill out on one of the golden sand beaches.

Day 2

Tremiti Islands 1. Join a cycling or hiking tour to explore the beautiful 15,000-acre Foresta Umbra.

Day 3

Tremiti Islands 2. Take a ferry from Vieste to the glorious Tremiti Islands (note that there are no ferries from Vieste off season). These bite-sized isles are still largely unspoilt despite many summer visitors. Renowned for dazzling blue-green waters and a fascinating coastline of sun-bleached cliffs, grottoes and rocky coves they are perfect for diving, swimming and boat trips. Explore historic sights at San Nicola, then take a boat to the pine-clad San Domino.

Day 4

Trani. Drive south along the coast to Trani, a beautiful port and fishing village with a prosperous air. The showpiece is the dazzling white Cathedral, set dramatically against the deep blue sea. Discover the historic quarter and colourful port with bars and restaurants.

OF **PUGLIA**

Day 5

Valle d'Itria. Discover the white towns and the *trulli* of the Itria Valley. Head south to Alberobello, capital of *trulli*, with around 1,500 of the quaint conical-roofed dwellings. Less touristy is the lovely hilltop towns of Locorotondo or Ostuni to the east. Spend an evening in the beautiful Baroque town of Martina Franca south of Alberobello. Join the *passeggiata*, dine in the historic centre and check out the evening cultural programme in this lively university town.

Days 6 & 7

Lecce. Head south to Lecce and stay a couple of days (the *Santa Chiara* is a charming hotel in the centre). This is the Baroque jewel of Puglia so spend time strolling the squares and streets of the old town, absorbing the exuberant facades of churches and palazzi. Combine culture with a spot of retail therapy checking out the *cartapesta* (papier-mâché) workshops and the chic shops selling olive oil and local pasta, then dine on the fashionable *cucina povera* (food for the poor) at Alle Due Corti.

Day 8

Otranto. Drive south to the lovely port of Otranto, ending your tour on the Adriatic coast. Visit the unique Romanesque cathedral with a remarkable floor mosaic, enjoy seafood specialities at *L'Altro Baffo* and spend the rest of the day relaxing on one of the fine sandy beaches.

CONTENTS

OVERVIEW	10
HISTORY AND CULTURE	15
OUT AND ABOUT	27

The Gargano Peninsula
Foresta Umbra 28, Monte Sant'Angelo 28, Vieste 30, Peschici 31, Rodi Garganico 32, Isole Tremiti 33, Il Tavoliere 36

27

Puglia Imperiale
Castel del Monte 38, The Coast 39, Barletta 39, Canne della Battaglia 40, Canosa di Puglia 41, Trani 42

37

Bari and beyond
Bari 46, Polignano a Mare 49

45

Valle d'Itria
Grotte di Castellana 53, Alberobello 53, Locorotondo 54, Martina Franca 55, Cisternino 58, Ostuni 59

52

The Salento
Brindisi 61, Lecce 63, The Grecia Salentina 68, Otranto 70, South from Otranto 72, Santa Maria di Leuca 73, Gallipoli 74, Taranto 77

60

An excursion to Matera
'City of Shame' 81, Seeing the city 81, The Sassi 83, The New Town 85, Parco della Murgia Materana 85

80

THINGS TO DO	87
Sports	87
Shopping	91
Entertainment	96
Children	97

FOOD AND DRINK	**100**
TRAVEL ESSENTIALS	**117**
WHERE TO STAY	**135**
INDEX	**142**

HIGHLIGHTS

A Pyrrhic Victory	18
Important Dates	25
Padre Pio	33
Diving and boat trips	36
Frederick II	40
Trulli Extraordinary	54
Capocollo di Martina Franca	57
Museo Archeologico Faggiano	67
Olive trees in peril	69
The Great Apulian Aqueduct	75
The Tarantella	79
Christ Stopped at Eboli	85
Pasta perfect	94
Calendar Of Events	99
Ricci di Mare	103

A NOTE TO READERS

At Rough Guides, we always strive to bring you the most up-to-date information. This book was produced during a period of continuing uncertainty caused by the Covid-19 pandemic, so please note that content is more subject to change than usual. We recommend checking the latest restrictions and official guidance.

OVERVIEW

Twenty years ago few foreign tourists took any interest in the heel of Italy's boot and many had never heard of Puglia. Northern Italians tended to regard the region, along with most of the Mezzogiorno (southern Italy) as a land somewhat apart from the rest of Italy, lacking the cultural riches of the north. But from a backward and neglected region Puglia has become the rising star of the south. Most of its tourists are Italian, but an increasing number of foreign Italophiles have been discovering the delights of this southern tip of Italy: from the Foresta Umbra and the sands of Gargano to the hilltop towns of the Valle d'Istria to the Baroque splendour of Lecce. The region is a vast natural larder, the plains and hillsides yielding huge quantities of wine, olive oil and durum wheat, the coasts producing superb fish and seafood. Eating out, whether in a seaside taverna or at a street stall, is one of the great pleasures of this region.

THE LAND OF THE TWO SEAS

Known as the 'land of the two seas', Puglia has the longest coastline of any region in Italy. Lapped by the Ionian Sea to the west and the Adriatic to the east, it stretches southwards from the 'spur' of the Gargano peninsula to the tip of the heel of the Italian boot. Most of the region is flat and fertile, with the large plain or *'Tavoliere'* of wheat fields around Foggia and further south great swathes of vineyards and silvery-green olive groves. The notable exception to the flat terrain is the spectacular and mountainous Gargano peninsula where dramatic limestone cliffs plunge into limpid blue waters. The interior of the peninsula is thickly wooded and attracts hikers and bikers, while the pale golden sands are a magnet for beach-lovers. Offshore lie the Isole Tremiti, a small archipelago of tiny islands surrounded by sparkling seas.

Wildflowers outside the hilltop town of Ostuni

Although it requires a fertile imagination to envisage the famous Roman battles on the plains of Puglia, there are plenty of reminders of the region's long and complex history. Temple ruins and treasures in Taranto's museum are reminders of the golden Greek era; while in Salento some villages have Greek names and roots. From the Roman era there are ruins of amphitheatres, from Norman times castles and cathedrals and from Spanish rule a wealth of Baroque.

TRULY TRULLI

On a domestic level the most distinctive and symbolic building of Puglia is the *trullo*, a small, quaint, cone-shaped structure whose origins may go back as far as the Middle Ages. These hobbit-like dwellings crop up in the countryside in the Istrian Valley and en masse in Alborebello. Designated a UNESCO World Heritage site, the town boasts over 1000 *trulli*. The region of the Valle d'Istria is also

Baia delle Zagare, in the Gargano Peninsula

home to the so-called *citta biancha*, or white towns, which crown the hilltops, their dominant cathedrals rising in the distance. Once you arrive in their historic centres (having braved the sprawling outskirts and the challenge of finding a parking space) it is less about specific sights than strolling through a maze of whitewashed alleys, discovering intimate *osterias* or enticing little *salumerias* selling culinary delights.

Almost as iconic as *trulli* are the ancient *masserie*, originally farms that were fortified to ward off invading Turks. Many of these have been stylishly converted to hotels and are very much part of the rapid rise in Puglia's tourism. Often in remote – or seemingly remote – locations, set amid vineyards, olive groves or woodland, they range from simple and affordable *agriturismi*-style farmhouses, where pigs, donkeys and hens graze freely in the grounds, to sophisticated five-star hotels with suites in villas, several swimming pools, beach club, spa – along with sky-high prices.

A SLOW PACE

When tourism took off in Puglia the region was proclaimed 'the new Tuscany' and the southern city of Lecce was billed 'the Florence of the south'. Anyone familiar with Tuscany might find the comparisons somewhat far-fetched. The parched and predominantly flat landscape of Puglia is a far cry from Tuscany's green and immaculate hills, and while Lecce boasts a riot of Baroque, you won't find Puglian Gothic or Renaissance churches, chapels or *palazzi*. This southern region moreover has a very slow pace of life and a rural simplicity, unchanged by time. Tuscany is more about culture, in Puglia you can seek it out but you can also feel fine about *la dolce far niente* – the enjoyment of idleness. This could be napping by the pool, putting a toe in the Adriatic, watching the *passeggiata* (evening stroll), feasting on freshly caught fish or downing a glass or two of Primitivo wine in the local bar.

Puglia may have lured celebrities (Justin Timberlake and Jessica Biel celebrated their wedding here, Helen Mirren and Meryl Street have country houses in Salento), but don't expect the sophistication and picture-postcard perfection of Positano, Capri or Sardinia's Costa Smeralda. Although there are luxury *masserie* and some sublime beaches, there are also stretches of unsightly coastal development and a number of neglected towns or villages. Although you can find glamorous parties on Gallipoli's beaches, nightlife is generally low-key and eateries tend to be small family-run tavernas rather than sophisticated restaurants. Parts of Puglia are quite wild and underdeveloped. It can still feel remote, but in the very best sense of the word.

A FOODIE HEAVEN

The region has a tradition of 'la cucina povera' (poor cuisine) which means remarkably flavoursome dishes based on an abundance of fresh, local and seasonal ingredients. The diet is a very simple, healthy one, based on abundant vegetables, fruit, fresh fish, top-quality olive oil and healthy pasta made with durum flour.

Puglia or Apulia?

Apulia is the old Latin name for the region, still sometimes used by English speakers. Locals and all other Italians call it *Puglia*, the modern Latin name, or sometimes the plural, topographical *Le Puglie*, as in *Il Tavoliere delle Puglie*, the vast plain in the north of the region.

'Seasonal', 'slow food' and 'farm-to-table' are not new to the food scene – it's how things have been for centuries. The signature pasta is *orechiette* or 'little ears' which you can see being made by hand in the backstreets of old Bari. The classic and hugely popular dish is *orecchiette alle cime di rapa,* translated as *orecchiette* with turnip tops but actually more like a leafy broccoli. Even those who don't like their greens admit to enjoying the dish. With 800km (497 miles) of coastline, it's not surprising that seafood is an essential element of Puglia's cuisine. You can feast on raw sea urchins straight from fishing boats, tuck into bowls of clams or mussels or savour steamed octopus or stuffed cuttlefish.

Climate is a key factor if you're considering visiting Puglia. The mid-summer heat can be relentless and the resorts impossibly crowded. Ideally visit in late spring and autumn, when it's warm with fewer tourists and peaceful beaches. If you have no choice but to go in high season do as the locals: enjoy a four-hour siesta, join the *passeggiata* as the towns reawaken and dine late in the company of Pugliesi. After all this is the Mezzogiorno where the locals are welcoming and the pace of life is delightfully slow.

COVID-19

Inevitably Puglia is facing a broad range of challenges caused by Covid-19. The economy relies on tourism and the region has taken a big hit from the pandemic, with restaurants, hotels, B&Bs and other tourist-related businesses closing down – and some for good. At the time of writing travel rules to Italy, including testing and quarantining, were tightening and anyone planning a visit should check on the current regulations. Those from the UK can find all the information at https://www.gov.uk/foreign-travel-advice/italy/entry-requirements. Details are also available on the Italian Tourist Board site at www.italia.it/en/Covid19.

HISTORY AND CULTURE

A BRIEF HISTORY
Between East and West, with long and exposed coastlines on either side, Puglia has always been vulnerable to attack and invasion. Ever since the arrival of seafarers from across the Adriatic Sea, foreign powers have fought for a stake here and made their mark. The Greeks and Romans, Lombards and Normans, Angevins and Aragonese, Habsburgs and Bourbons have all vied for control, leaving behind a beguiling cultural hybrid.

MAGNA GRAECIA
It was during the Bronze Age, from around 1700BC, that the Greeks first established links with southern Italy, the Mycenaeans from mainland Greece and the Minoans from Crete forming trading links. But it was another four centuries or so before Greek settlers founded colonies in southern Italy. Exiles from Sparta founded Taras (modern Taranto), which became the most prosperous town in Magna Graecia in the 3rd century BC and a focus of Greek culture. Other Greek city states were founded at Hydrus (Otranto) and Kallipolis (Gallipoli). Little remains of this golden era although a pair of columns from Taranto's Doric Temple survive and there is a veritable treasure trove of finds from ancient Tara in the city's superb Archaeological Museum.

Altamura Man
The oldest human remains discovered in Puglia are those of the calcified Altamura Man, discovered in a karst sinkhole in the Grotta di Lamalunga near Altamura. Recent tests show that the fossil (which is still in the cave) is that of a Neanderthal man, who died between 128,000 and 187,000 years ago.

Statue of Zeus from Ugento, 5th century BC

ROMAN RULE

By the time the Romans were advancing from the north, Magna Graecia had been weakened by wars between the city states and invasions by Etruscans. The Romans rapidly expanded throughout the region. Taras (Taranto) rebelled against the Romans and sought the military assistance of Pyrrhus, King of Epirus (see box) in north-western Greece. After early defeats at the hands of the King, Rome defeated the Tarentines and occupied Taranto in 272BC. They rapidly colonised and Latinized the region and by 266BC, when the Romans took Brundisium (modern Brindisi), the whole of southern Italy had come under their control.

During the Second Punic War Hannibal invaded Italy (218BC), crossing the Alps and establishing a hold over the north of Italy. Reinforced by Gallic tribesmen he marched south, and in 216BC annihilated a huge Roman army at the celebrated Battle of Cannae. Carthaginian forces remained in Puglia whilst Hannibal attempted to forge sufficient Italian alliances to make good a permanent occupation of Italy. He failed in the enterprise and was forced to retreat to Africa where Rome defeated Carthage at Zama in 202BC, bringing an end to the war.

Rome then ruled the whole of the peninsula for some six centuries. Puglia was unified and acquired great importance with all the trade routes to eastern Mediterranean countries converging on the region through the port of Brindisi and along the Appian and Trajan ways. Today Roman remains are dotted across Puglia, including the columns terminating the Appian Way at Brindisi and the large amphitheatre and Roman theatre at Lecce.

THE DARK AGES

Following the fall of the Roman Empire in the west in 476AD, there was a long, dark age for Italy with successive invasions by barbarians. These were temporarily arrested by the Byzantine reconquest of Sicily. In 535 the forces of the eastern Emperor Justinian under the command of Belisarius fought a succession of campaigns against the Goths. In 536 Belisarius crossed to the mainland. Most of southern Italy welcomed the Byzantine army, but the reconquest was curtailed by Lombard invaders

The Roman theatre in Lecce

who descended from the north and confined the Byzantines to the extreme south.

The next wave of invaders were the Saracens from North Africa, including Arabs, Spanish Muslims and Berbers. Sicily was under entire effective Saracen control by the end of the 9th century and the island was used as the main base for invasions which laid waste to much of the land and buildings of Puglia. Short-lived emirates were established at Bari and Taranto.

The eastern Empire continued to rule parts of the mainland south and in 975 began a successful military campaign of further re-conquest. Effective Byzantine imperial rule was established over the whole of Puglia, as well as Calabria and Basilicata. This resulted

A PYRRHIC VICTORY

The English expression 'Pyrrhic Victory' – a victory gained at too great a cost – originates from the warlike activities of King Pyrrhus, an ancient Greek warrior, in Puglia. When Rome was asserting dominion over southern Italy, Pyrrhus championed the Greek cause and met the Roman army at Asculum, winning his famous victory in 279BC by the deployment of elephants. The losses on either side are unknown but Pyrrhus is said to have commented '*If we are victorious in one more battle with Rome we shall be utterly ruined.*' His offer of peace to the Romans on condition that they evacuated all southern Italy was rejected by the Senate, leading to further martial conflict; but such were the Greek losses that Pyrrhus retreated back to his Kingdom of Epirus in 275BC, leaving the Romans masters of all Italy. One city, Tarentum (Taranto), remained Greek, a reminder that much of the 'Greek Salento' of today owes its name to the ancient period when Puglia was Greek, not Roman – or Italian as we know it.

in tremendous waves of Greek settlers who were arriving from the east so that by the end of the 10th and early 11th centuries Puglia was, to a large extent, culturally Greek.

NORMAN CONQUEST

The earliest Normans to come to Puglia were knights on pilgrimage to Christian shrines, most notably to St Michael at Monte Sant'Angelo in the Gargano. This gradually gave

The Norman fleet of Roger II de Hauteville

rise to Papal encouragement of a Norman military invasion by the Hauteville dynasty from northern France, to drive out the Byzantines. This Papal-Norman alliance led to the annexation of Sicily and large parts of southern Italy including Puglia. The celebrated Crusader Robert de Hauteville (c1015-85), who was nicknamed 'Guiscard' or 'the Crafty', ousted Lombards, Saracens and Byzantines and became Duke of Apulia, Calabria and Sicily. In 1130 Roger II of the Hauteville dynasty was crowned the first king of Sicily. His holdings included most of southern Italy and his court was one of the wealthiest that existed in the entire world. Puglia benefited from the peace and security of the times. Norman rule also left an indelible stamp on Puglia with the construction of both castles and monuments and also magnificent cathedrals, too. Puglia's port cities transformed into harbours for the Crusades and as a result enjoyed a flourishing trade with the Levant.

STUPOR MUNDI

In the late 12th century the Norman dynasty was replaced by the German House of Hohenstaufen, bringing Sicily and southern Italy within the sway of the Holy Roman Emperor. The Hohenstaufen Holy Roman Emperor Henry VI was succeeded by his son Frederick II when he died in 1197. Known as Stupor Mundi or Wonder of the World, Frederick (1194–1250) was one of the most significant rulers of the middle ages. At European level he claimed pre-eminence over all other secular rulers and struggled to wrest from the papacy its burgeoning political power and return it to its true Christian ethos of, as he saw it, purity and saintliness. He introduced a unified legal system, promoted the arts and sciences and encouraged a blend of Islamic, Jewish and Christian cultures. He left his mark with 29 castles in Puglia, including his enduring monument, the Castel del Monte.

> **Saracen siege**
>
> In 1480 a Turkish fleet with some 18,000 soldiers laid siege to Otranto, slaughtering the majority of males over 15. Around 800 of the survivors were offered mercy if they renounced the Christian faith. They refused and were beheaded. Their relics are preserved in the Chapel of Martyrs in Otranto's Cathedral.

FRENCH AND SPANISH

The death of Frederick II in 1250 marked the end of the Hohenstaufen dynasty and the beginning of a long period of decline for Puglia under various foreign rulers. The Hohenstaufen were succeeded by the Angevins, a ruling dynasty from central France, followed by the Spanish House of Aragon. In Puglia the economy declined, the population decreased and many towns and villages were abandoned. Under the Spaniards (1503–1707) trade

FRENCH AND SPANISH

suffered from heavy taxes, corruption was rife among Spanish officials and landowners exploited the common people.

The death in 1700 of the childless Charles II of Spain, who was the last of the Spanish Habsburgs, prompted the War of the Spanish Succession (1700–1715). Under the Treaty of Utrecht in 1713 southern Italy was ceded to the Austrian Habsburgs. The arrangement only lasted until 1738 when the Bourbon King Charles VII expelled the Austrians and established the Two Kingdoms of Sicily as an independent kingdom under the Bourbon dynasty.

In the early 19th century Puglia, like most of the rest of Italy, was controlled by Napoleonic France. Although French occupation lasted only nine years (1805–14), it was a period of economic and agricultural reform not previously seen even in post-medieval

Sixteenth-century map of Gallipoli

times. After the fall of Napoleon the Kingdom of the Two Sicilies reverted to the Bourbons after the Congress of Vienna. While under the earlier Bourbon monarchs the region had seen some significant progress industrially, by its last decade Bourbon rule was despised for its oppression. The continued unrest set the stage for Garibaldi, leader of the Risorgimento and the campaign for Unification.

FROM UNIFICATION TO PRESENT

With his so-called 'Thousand' (volunteers) Garibaldi sailed into Sicily in 1860 and from there into southern Italy, heralding the flight of the last Bourbon, Francis II, from Naples. In 1861 Vittorio Emanuele II was proclaimed king and the region became part of the Kingdom of Italy. But southern Italians were soon disillusioned

Taranto life in the 18th century

with life as part of a new unified Italy. Taxes rose, the economy declined and only one percent of the population was eligible to vote. There were abortive uprisings, some savagely repressed. The only escape from poverty seemed to be emigration and in the last decades of the 19th century enormous numbers of southern Italians sought a new life overseas, mainly in North or South America.

Trulli dwellers in Alberobello in the 1940s

It was not until after World War I that Puglia saw any stability or prosperity. The malaria crisis which had ravaged Italy, particularly the south, was finally brought under control, though was not completely eradicated until the 1960s. Poor farming conditions and domestic discomfort, brought about by the parched terrain, was greatly alleviated by the Great Aqueduct in 1939 (see page 75) and then by modern wells cut deep into the rocks.

During the 1950s and 60s, unemployment led to another mass migration, with southerners leaving to find jobs in northern Italy, which was enjoying an economic boom, and also to other parts of Europe. The trend declined as economic conditions improved in the south. Today Puglia is a far more productive area, both agriculturally and industrially. Thanks to its huge production of wheat and pasta it became known as the breadbasket of Italy. It produces 40 percent of the country's olive oil and is one of the largest wine-making regions in Italy. Small food-processing

Olive oil is big business

industries are widespread, but the main industrial centres are Bari and Taranto. Albeit on a smaller scale than before, migration is still an issue with young Pugliesi (and southern Italians in general), particularly the well-educated. Youth-unemployment is high and many ambitious young Italians are discouraged by the scarcity of jobs, particularly the most rewarding ones, not to mention *clientelismo* – political patronage and nepotism. Meanwhile waves of migrants have been arriving on southern Italian shores, including Puglia, despite the fact that migrant rescue ships are currently banned from docking in Italy.

In the first decade of the 21st century low-cost carriers opened up the region to British tourists and the meteoric rise in visitor numbers had a highly beneficial effect on Puglia's economy. The region has seen the rejuvenation of historic centres, the restoration of museums and the transformation of manor farms into luxury accommodation.

But in 2020 and 2021 the Covid-19 pandemic broke out and as a result, it wreaked havoc on tourism around the region, with a dramatic decline in the numbers of visitors. On the plus side Puglia is set to be the biggest beneficiary of the Italian share of the EU's €750 billion fund to boost the economy and recover from the Covid-19 fallout.

IMPORTANT DATES

700,000 BC Paleolithic Man inhabits caves such as the Grotta dei Cervi.
3rd / 2nd millennium BC Messapians migrate from Dalmatia to Puglia.
8th century BC Greek colonists establish Taras (Taranto) and other cities.
275 BC Roman defeat of Greeks at Beneventum, last battle of the Pyrrhic War.
216 BC Hannibal defeats Romans at Cannae.
190BC Romans extend Via Appia to Brindisi.
476 AD Fall of western Roman empire. Gothic tribes invade.
6th century Byzantine re-conquest of parts of Italy including Puglia.
9th century Saracen invasions from Sicily destroy parts of Puglia.
1130 Norman invader Roger II rules southern Italy.
1220 Holy Roman Emperor Frederick II starts his 30-year domination of the region.
1266–1282 Angevin rule in southern Italy.
1282–1500 Spain, France and the Papacy vie for control over southern Italy.
1501 King Ferdinand of Spain incorporates southern Italy including Puglia into his Habsburg empire.
1713 Treaty of Utrecht: Austria inherits Habsburg lands including southern Italy.
1738 Treaty of Vienna: Puglia passes to the Spanish house of Bourbon.
1860 Unification process brings the end of Bourbon rule.
1880–1915 Massive exodus from southern Italy to the New World.
1950–60s Mass migration from southern to northern Italy, and Europe.
2018 Italian general election. Hung Parliament leads to a coalition.
2019 Matera (in Basilicata) is European Capital of Culture. Migrants continue to reach Italy's southern shores.
2020 In March Bergamo in Lombardy becomes the European epicentre of Covid-19. Italy suffers one of Europe's highest death rates.
2021 Mario Draghi, former President of the European Central Bank, is invited to form a national unity government. Italy receives its first payment from the EU's €750 billion recovery fund.

Vieste, beautifully set on a tip of the Gargano Peninsula

OUT AND ABOUT

The 'land of two seas', Puglia stretches 400km (248 miles) from north to south, between the Ionian and Adriatic seas. A car is the best way to get around but you would need at least three weeks to take in all the highlights. The majority of visitors arrive at the capital, Bari, explore the whitewashed hill villages and *trulli* of the Valle d'Itria and then head south to the Salentine Peninsula. Those with more time can take in the alluring but less accessible Gargano promontory in the north of the region. The chapter starts here and moves south along the coast to Bari, through the Valle d'Itria to the Baroque city of Lecce and the coastal towns and beaches of Salento. Last but not least is the city of Matera, the jewel of the region of Basilicata, just across the border from Puglia.

THE GARGANO PENINSULA

The only real mountains of Puglia are clustered on the Gargano promontory, a thickly forested peninsula that juts out into the Adriatic to form 'the spur' of the boot of Italy. This is one of Italy's most beautiful regions, discovered but not wrecked by tourism. The coastline is spectacular: craggy, bleached limestone cliffs, pale sandy beaches, grottoes, rocky coves and beguiling blue-green waters. In contrast is the thickly wooded wild interior, where only dappled light penetrates the trees.

For most foreign tourists the Gargano is still regarded as rather out of the way. The road from sprawling Manfredónia, gateway to the promontory, is very slow-going, whether you opt for the serpentine coastline or the hairpin bends through the mountains. From Bari airport it takes at least 2 hours 30 minutes by car to the main resort of Vieste. In July and August large numbers of northern Italians flock here – and to the lovely little Tremiti islands offshore. Outside these months it's relatively quiet. By October, when it is normally still warm and the sea water averages 20°C, many tourist amenities have closed down completely and don't get going again until late spring.

FORESTA UMBRA

In the heart of the Gargano National Park the **Foresta Umbra** ❶ is an ancient 15,000-acre forest of beech, chestnut, Aleppo pines and oaks. The only true forested area in Puglia, this protected region is the habitat of deer, foxes and hares and is home to most of the varieties of orchids indigenous to Europe. The forest has marked trails and is becoming increasingly popular for guided hiking and cycling tours.

MONTE SANT'ANGELO

The Gargano's best-known medieval town is **Monte Sant'Angelo** ❷, a remarkable little pilgrimage town, which was designated a World Heritage site in 2011. It perches on a rocky spur at 800m (2,625ft) and affords jaw-dropping views over the Bay of Manfredónia. Whether you're a worshipper or not, it's well worth the journey up tortuous bends to see the old quarter with its picturesque alleys and monuments. Avoid Sundays and on no account go on the 29th September, St Michael's Day, when thousands of pilgrims flock to the hilltop, some climbing all the way up on foot from Vieste. Their target is the fifth-century **Santuario di San Michele** (www.santuariosanmichele.it; 7.30am–7.30pm, shorter hours off season), located in a grotto where the archangel is said to have appeared three times to the Bishop of Siponto. From the double-arched Gothic portico, flanked by an octagonal belfry, a staircase of 86 steps takes you down to the dimly lit

Santuario di San Michele

sanctuary. The cave is entered through a pair of beautiful bronze doors, depicting biblical scenes and believed to have been cast in Constantinople. Inside the grotto are a 16th-century statue of the Archangel and a 12th-century marble episcopal throne.

Opposite the Sanctuary steps lead down to the **Tomba di Rotari** (April–Oct 9am–noon and 3–7pm, Nov–March to 4.30pm). Originally believed to be a Lombard tomb, it is now thought to be a 12th-century baptistry. Entry is via the remains of the medieval Chiesa di San Pietro, destroyed in a 19th-century earthquake. At the uppermost part of the town is the much-modified Norman **castle**, with fine views and one surviving tower, the Torre dei Giganti.

From Mattinata to Vieste the inland road climbs up steeply for about 18km (11 miles), and for the next 24km (15 miles) twists downwards through the wild landscape before reaching Vieste. The much slower coastal road, via beaches and tourists resorts, has

THE GARGANO PENINSULA

some fabulous stretches of sands, including the **Baia delle Zagere**, an exquisite crescent of white sand beach, with two large rocks rising from turquoise waters.

VIESTE

The largest resort in the region, **Vieste** ❸ is beautifully set on a tip of the Gargano Peninsula, surrounded by caves, cliffs and golden-beaches. Among its attractions are the boat trips, skirting the cave-riddled coast, and excursions across to the Isole Tremiti (Tremiti Islands, see page 33). Tourist development dominates the outskirts of Vieste but the town has a charming historic quarter of whitewashed houses, medieval alleys and arches. The dominant monuments are the Romanesque **cathedral**, remodelled over the centuries, and the **castle** (closed to the public), built by Frederick

Spiaggia di Pizzomunno and its monolith

ll at the highest point of the town.

Vieste is famous for its beaches. Two of the best are the spacious **Spiaggia di Pizzomunno**, south of the resort, named after the 20-metre (66ft)-high rock monolith rising from the sands and the huge **Spiaggia di Scialmarino**, 4.5km (3 miles) to the north. There are also beaches within walking distances. As in most Puglian resorts the larger swathes of sand are blanketed with regimented rows of sun-loungers and parasols but after August everything, including the tourists, seems to disappear.

The trabucchi of Gargano

On the rocks between Vieste, Peschici and Rodi Garganico, look out for the dozen or so wooden contraptions suspended over the sea, known as *trabucchi*. Traditionally used for fishing, these consist of a large platform and long wooden poles, beams, ropes and pulleys to lower nets into the water and bring them up with the catch. Some of the *trabucchi* have been restored and three of them have been converted into enticing sea-view restaurants.

PESCHICI

From Vieste the SS 89 winds through olive groves, then snakes its way up into the wooded mountains before descending to Peschici. A stop at the roadside stalls selling cheese, olive oil and chillies will make a welcome break from the hairpin bends. Perched high above the sea **Peschici** ❹ is a charming fishing town where white houses tumble down the cliffside. More intimate than Vieste, the seaside resort has a lively little *centro storico*, a hilltop castle and dozens of inviting outlets for local Pugliese products, including the highly regarded local olive oil. You can learn all about it at **Al Vecchio Frantoio** which has an old olive press and quality extra-virgin

Peschici

olive oils (lemon-flavoured is a speciality), along with explanations and tastings. From here the cobbled street leads up to **Castello di Peschici** (June–Sept 9.30am–1pm, 4.30–8.30pm), dating back to the 10th century but much remodelled. The ground floor, formerly used as a prison and arms depot, is now a museum with a gruesome collection of torture devices.

Ferries from Peschici depart daily in season for the Isole Tremiti. Another option is a coastal boat trip to see bizarrely shaped and fancifully named grottoes, quiet coves and secluded beaches. Taking a dip in the pristine sea is always an option.

RODI GARGANICO

The SS89 continues its scenic switchback route through the mountains, cutting through forests of lush pines, then dropping down to the sprawling, non-descript resort of San Menaio. The beach stretches all the way to **Rodi Garganico** ❺ which, like Vieste and Peschici, is picturesquely set on a headland with houses built up on the spur. It is more down to earth than Vieste or Peschici and a railway divides the sea from the town, but the old centre has plenty of charm. Steep streets, where washing flaps in the breeze, lead up to the historic centre with its quiet cobbled streets and spacious main piazza. The resort has some lovely white beaches but you would be hard-pushed to find space here in July or August.

East of Rodi Garganico lie two coastal, fish-filled lakes, Lesino and Varano, separated from the sea by sand dunes. These are both popular with birdwatchers, who come to see species on the Africa–Europe migratory route.

ISOLE TREMITI

An archipelago in the Adriatic Sea, 22km (14 miles) north of the Gargano Peninsula, the **Isole Tremiti** ❻ are renowned for their natural beauty and dazzling clear waters. *'Tremiti'* means 'tremors'

PADRE PIO

From a medieval farming hamlet, San Giovanni Rotondo, west of Manfredónia, has become a global centre of pilgrimage visited by around seven million visitors a year. Perched on a hill and accessed via a twisting road, the town is inextricably linked with the Capuchin friar, Padre Pio (1887–1968), a stigmatist and miracle-worker who lived and worked here as a healer of the sick for 52 years. Father Pio was proclaimed a saint in 2002 and is worshipped across the region. His remains lie in the crypt of the Convent of Santa Maria delle Grazie, which was enlarged in the late 1950s to accommodate the overflow of pilgrims. By the Millennium space was again at a premium and the leading Italian architect, Renzo Piano, was commissioned to build a new church. It is only 16 metres (52ft) high but has capacity for 6,500 worshippers, one of the largest in Italy. There are no less than five annual festivals celebrating the life of the saint. His image is ubiquitous, in bars, shops and garages, and the favourite souvenirs are kitsch little Padre Pios.

34　THE GARGANO PENINSULA

and derives from the islands' renowned seismic activity. This has also characterized their landscape: jagged white cliffs, sandy coves and sparkling grottoes along the coastline. Only two of the five are inhabited and the population is around 200.

The islands have traditionally been a place of exile. Caesar Augustus banished his granddaughter, Julia the Younger, to San Domino for her promiscuity and Charlemagne had his father-in-law, accused of conspiracy, sent here after removing his eyes and limbs. The islands were used as a penal colony in the 19th century and in 1938 Mussolini banished hundreds of homosexuals to an internment camp on San Domino.

The islands can be reached by ferry service from May to September from Manfredonia, Vieste, Peschici and Rodi Garganico. (The only year-round service to the islands is from Termoli, on the coast of Molise.) There is also an affordable helicopter service (€50 return, 20-minute journey) to San Domino from Foggia (www.alidaunia.it). Cars are not permitted on the islands. The ferry trip alone is worthwhile, especially from Vieste, where you can enjoy stunning views of the coast with its white cliffs and beaches before the boat heads out to the islands.

View to San Nicola

San Nicola

The fast *aliscafi* (hydrofoils) from Gargano normally

arrive at the rocky little island of **San Nicola**, with its picturesque port and colourful fishing boats beached on the pebble shore. From here you can take a boat trip around the islands and be dropped off at San Domino, returning to San Nicola on one of the hourly ferries. Alternatively there are water taxis between the islands.

Benedictine monks founded the Abbey on San Nicola in 1010 which by the 13th century had amassed great wealth. In 1412 it was fortified to withstand attacks from the Turks. In 1782 the abbey was suppressed by King Ferdinand IV of Naples and transformed into a penal colony. From the port of San Nicola take the steep path up to the battlements leading to the graceful Romanesque-style Church of Santa Maria a Mare. Founded in 1045 and remodelled over the centuries, the church has a beautiful portal, a 11th–12th-century mosaic pavement and a wooden Byzantine cross. Beyond the church you can wander among cloisters, overgrown ruins and ancient Greek tombs, all the while enjoying panoramic views of the islands.

Up to San Nicola's battlements

San Domino

The largest and greenest of the islands, San Domino lacks the old world charm of San Nicolo but has beautiful secluded coves, a fine white-sand beach and a handful of hotels, villas and restaurants.

THE GARGANO PENINSULA

The Benedectine monks called this island Paradise Orchard thanks to its fertility, profusion of flowers and shady woods. From its fragrant pine-clad slopes there are fine views of the pristine seas.

IL TAVOLIERE

In stark contrast to the mountainous Gargano Peninsula are the vast, flat wheatlands of **Il Tavoliere** ❼ stretching west from the Gargano massif to the foothills of the Apennines. This is also an industrial area and the towns have limited appeal to tourists. **Foggia** ❽, the capital of the eponymous province, is rarely visited by tourists but retains a Romanesque cathedral, remodelled in the 18th century. **Lucera** ❾ has Puglia's only Gothic cathedral in southern Italy, as well as the ruins of Frederick II's largest castle; **Troia** ❿, the most attractive town of the region, has a remarkable

DIVING AND BOAT TRIPS

The unbelievably translucent waters around the Tremiti islands offer some of the best diving and snorkelling in southern Italy. The uninhabited and protected little island of Capraia, with its quiet coves, is one of the best diving spots, particularly at Punta Secca and Cala dei Turchi. On a 14m (46ft) -deep seabed near the islet a statue of Padre Pio (see page 33) was submerged in 1998. The small boats which take tourists around the islands stop here so they can dive down to see the statue. However, unless the sea is really calm, it's not always easy for the boatman to locate the statue. The boats also skirt the craggy limestone cliffs of San Domino, which are pitted with fascinating caves. One of the most famous is the Grotta delle Viole, where in spring the rocks are covered by caper flowers that look like wild violets (*viole*). Inside the water's hues and clarity defy description.

Cycling in Il Tavoliere

cathedral with a successful fusion of Pisan-Romanesque architecture and Byzantine Saracen-inspired ornament.

PUGLIA IMPERIALE

The region extending west from Bari is known as Puglia Imperiale, on account of the legacy of Frederick II, the dominant figure in Puglia's long and varied history. This is a land of castles, cathedrals and historic cities. The Castel del Monte, dominating the countryside around Andria, is a supreme example of the 29 castles which Frederick built in Puglia. Along the coast the seaside stunner is Trani, known as 'the pearl of Puglia' and boasting a dazzling white cathedral suspended between a sky and a sea that vie for brilliant blues.

A car is a best way to explore the region, particularly if you intend to visit Castel del Monte.

CASTEL DEL MONTE

Dominating the landscape, on a 540m (1,771ft)-high rocky peak, stands Frederick II's stronghold and retreat: the medieval **Castel del Monte** ⓫ (www.casteldelmonte.beniculturali.it; April–Sept 10am–6.45pm, last admission 6pm, Oct–March 9am–5.45pm, last admission 5pm; fee-paying shuttle service from car park to castle). The imposing structure had a unique design for the time: a perfectly proportioned octagonal plan with octagonal towers at each angle – possibly the influence of Middle Eastern architecture.

The monument has always been a puzzle for historians. Its thick 26m (85ft)-high walls and towers suggest it was part of Frederick's network of strategically placed defensive castles, yet it has no drawbridge, moat, arrow slits, dungeons for prisoners or other fortress features and the large marble rooms with mosaics, paintings and tapestries (treasures that were looted long ago) are more like those you would find in a lavish royal residence. Some experts suggest that the design was inspired by astronomy, a science known to have fascinated the cultured Frederick.

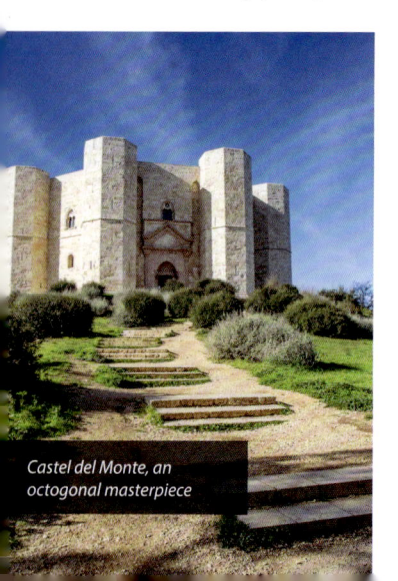

The castle served as a refuge for the noble families of nearby **Andria** ⓬ during the plague of 1665 and was later abandoned, becoming a hideout for brigands and

Castel del Monte, an octogonal masterpiece

political exiles. The state bought it in 1876, and three years later began a 40-year restoration programme. The site was awarded UNESCO World Heritage status in 1996. The interior is spartan but there are audio-guides to help you imagine the castle in former times.

> ### Castle on a coin
>
> If you're in Italy you may well have a picture of the Castel del Monte in your pocket. The castle is depicted on the reverse side of the Italian one euro cent coin.

THE COAST

As you come south from the Gargano peninsula the coast is flat with extensive salt flats at Margherita di Savoia. Producing over five million tons of salt a year these are among the largest in Europe. The protected wetlands along this coastline are of ornithological interest and have one of the largest colonies of pink flamingos in Europe.

BARLETTA

The first main town you come across is **Barletta** ⑬, a busy port and industrial centre. The town retains an historic centre with a handsome castle built by Frederick II, a Romanesque cathedral and, most famously, the **Colossus**, a bronze statue of a Byzantine emperor, more remarkable for its size (over 5m/16ft high) and age (over 1500 years old) than any aesthetic merit. It was reputedly stolen by Venetians from Constantinople but it was reported that the boat sank and the statue was washed ashore at Barletta. Behind the statue rises Barletta's most important church of all, the **Chiesa del Santo Sepolcro**, which is a remodelled Romanesque church that played an important role during the Crusades.

CANNE DELLA BATTAGLIA

A hill in the lower Ofanto valley, inland from Barletta, was the site of one of the most pivotal battles in classical history and one of the worst defeats ever suffered by the Roman army. Having already defeated two Roman armies during the Second Punic War, Hannibal based himself in the town of Cannae, making it his base to

> ### FREDERICK II
>
> As well as being King of Germany and Holy Roman Emperor, Frederick of Hohenstaufen (1194–1250) acquired the titles of King of Sicily, King of Italy, Holy Roman Emperor and King of Jerusalem. His mother was Constance of Altavilla, later to become Queen of Sicily, his father Henry VI of the Hohenstaufen dynasty. At the age of four Frederick became an orphan and was placed under the protection of Pope Innocent III. Styled *'Stupor Mundi'* (Wonder of the World), he took control of southern Italy in 1220 and became the most significant political and intellectual figure of 13th-century Europe. An enlightened ruler who waged a bitter and ultimately unsuccessful feud with the Papacy, he was also an avid sportsman whose brilliant treatise on falconry still ranks among the most accurate descriptions of the subject. Influenced by Arabic and Jewish learning and imbued with the eastern spirit of his age as well as the pragmatism of the Norman rulers who preceded him, Frederick brought to bear a unique unifying spirit in Sicily and southern Italy. Through his court he nurtured philosophy, poetry, mathematics and the natural sciences. In Puglia he struck such a chord with the people that he was nicknamed *'Puer Apuliae'* or Son of Apulia. Frederick left his mark on castles across the region and in particular on Castel del Monte, his own masterly fusion of poetry and mathematics in stone.

conquer southern Italy. On 2nd August 216 BC, an army of 86,000 Roman troops faced 40,000 Carthaginians at the site which is now called the **Canne della Battaglia** ⓮. Hannibal's brilliant use of tactics led to the virtual annihilation of the Roman fighting force. Seventy thousand Romans were killed, 4,500 taken prisoner. Nothing remains of the battleground, but the site is protected as the **Antiquarium** and **Parco**

Canne della Battaglia ruins

Archeologico di Canne della Battaglia (Wed–Sat 9am–5.15pm). The new Antiquarium documents the history of Cannae from Prehistory to the Middle Ages, with emphasis on the historical battle while the Archaeological Park reveals the remains of an ancient Daunian settlement, along with Roman, early Christian and medieval remains.

CANOSA DI PUGLIA

Further archaeological finds can be seen at **Canosa di Puglia** ⓯ 13km (8 miles) southwest of Canne della Battaglia, and nicknamed Little Rome because of its seven hills. Although a rather dreary town today it was a major city in Roman times. Archaeological finds, dispersed across the city and often tricky to access without a guide, include the Hypogea Lagrasta, a rock-hewn complex of underground tombs. The largest of the three hypogea has nine rooms and fragments of frescoes.

Cattedrale di San Sabino

Treasures within the town's five-domed **Cattedrale di San Sabino** (9am–noon, 3–7pm; free) include an 11th-century pulpit, the early 12th-century tomb of Bohemond I, Prince of Taranto, with magnificent bronze doors and the oldest bishop's throne in Apulia, carved by the 11th-century sculptor, Romualdo. The animal carvings show traces of Arab influence and the throne has been compared to an Islamic chess piece.

TRANI

Following the fall of Canosa to the Saracens in the 9th century, the fishing port of **Trani** ⓰ expanded and became one of the most important Italian trading centres, rivalling Bari as a commercial port. The iconic site is its cathedral, but this is just one of many monuments in Trani's beautifully restored historic centre. The town has a marked air of prosperity with streets of glistening marble cobbles, elegant boutiques, finely preserved *palazzi* and fashionable cafés and bars.

Cattedrale di San Nicola Pellegrino

The town's dominant and most dramatically located monument is the **Cattedrale di San Nicola Pellegrino** (Apr–Oct Mon–Sat 9am–12.30pm, 3.30–7pm, Sun 9am–12.30pm, 4–8.30pm, Nov–Mar closes 6pm and 8.30pm on Sun; charge only for campanile), one of the finest examples of Apulian-Romanesque architecture. It was founded at the end of the 11th century to house the remains of a young Greek pilgrim called Nicola who died in Trani. The portal is adorned with finely carved sculptures and frames bronze doors with 32 impressive reliefs. The restored original doors, carved by the 12th-century sculptor Barisano of Trani, who also cast the bronze doors of Ravello's Cathedral, are preserved inside the church.

The interior is divided into an upper and lower church. The upper was restored to its Romanesque design from the elaborate Baroque modelling it was given in 1837: it is narrow, lofty and light, bare of ornament, with two tiers and a beamed ceiling. Below is a crypt with a forest of pillars and a lower church adorned with 14th- and 15th-century frescoes. For those prepared to climb 258 steps there are fine views from the top of the 60m (170ft) -high Campanile.

Castello Svevo

Guarding the seashore just to the west of the cathedral piazza is the **Castello Svevo**, (Swabian Castle; Wed–Mon 8.30am–7.30pm). The castle was part of Frederick II's intense programme of demolition, restoration and building of fortifications, transforming Puglia from

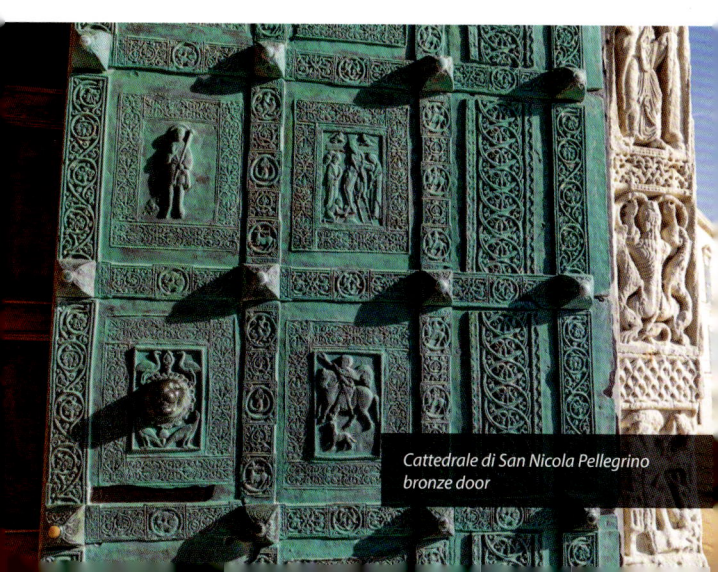

Cattedrale di San Nicola Pellegrino bronze door

a land of cathedrals to a land of castles. Built in 1233–49, with later alterations and heavy restoration, the castle has a square design, four large corner towers and a moat which once joined the sea. It served as a prison from the 19th century until 1975. Today it's a tourist sight and cultural centre but apart from a small museum, with finds from the restoration work, there is little to see inside.

Jewish Quarter

A stroll through the narrow alleys of Trani's historic centre will reveal medieval churches, handsome palazzi and two synagogues. Under Frederick II a large Jewish community flourished in Trani and the city had four active synagogues, but by 1380 all four had been converted to churches, and the remaining Jews were forced to convert to Christianity. Two synagogues survive.

The **Scolagrande** on Via La Giudea (the main street of the ancient Ghetto), later converted into the Chiesa di Sant'Anna, now houses the Jewish section of Trani's Diocesan Museum. Just to the south the **Scolanova** ('New Synagogue') became the Chiesa di Santa Maria in Scolanova. It was deconsecrated and returned to the Jewish community in 2006.

Chiesa di Ognissanti

A two-minute walk to the east, with its entrance on Via Ognissanti, is the simple and

Trani's elegant port

The Villa Communale, Trani's green oasis

evocative **Chiesa di Ognissanti** (Mon–Sat 9am–noon, Fri and Sat 4–8pm; free). Founded in the 12th century this recently restored church was said to have formerly been a Knights Templar church. Don't miss the lovely facade at the east end with the bell tower and three semicircular apses facing Trani's elegant little **port**. By day this is a picturesque scene of colourful fishing boats and yachts, whilst after dark it's the lively scene of the *passeggiata* (evening stroll) and abuzz with café and restaurant life. If you walk all the way round you come to the **Villa Comunale**, Trani's delightful public gardens.

BARI AND BEYOND

A major trading port since ancient times, Bari reached its zenith in the medieval era and by the 11th century was the most important Adriatic port. Today it is the capital of Puglia, the main point of

Bari Vecchia backstreet

arrival by air to the region and still a busy port with ferries serving Greece, Croatia and Albania. Tourists who arrive here rarely make time to see the city, unaware that it is no longer a down-at-heel port. Reinvented Bari has become a more welcoming, cosmopolitan city offering chic shopping and lively nightlife as well as history, culture and a fascinating historic centre. It even has its cuisine, *cucina barese*, with some great street food and seafood restaurants. Although the city is far safer than it used to be it's still wise to keep an eye on valuables as you stroll around the streets.

Bari is the gateway to Adriatic resorts and towns of central Puglia; it is also only an hour's drive from Matera in Basilicata (see page 80). A favourite excursion for the Baresi is the fashionable resort of Polignano a Mare, 34km (21 miles) south of the city (see page 49).

BARI

The city of **Bari** ⓱ consists of Bari Vecchia, or Old Bari, and the Città Nuova, or modern quarter, laid out on a grid plan with wide, straight avenues. The latter is the financial and administrative centre and the location of museums, theatres, concert halls and the university. Via Sparano is home to the famous fashion labels, Corso Cavour and Via Manzoni to the cheaper stores.

Bari Vecchia

Packed on a promontory between the old and new ports, **Bari Vecchia** is an atmospheric maze of medieval alleys, small courtyards, shrines and churches. The old town can be covered on foot; alternatively there are bicycles, Segways and scooters to rent – or tuk-tuks at the ready if you want a personal tour. Meandering around on foot it is easy to get lost in the tangle of streets but you are never far from a landmark. Delis and eateries proliferate: hole-in-the-wall grocery stores sell nuts and spices, small tavernas serve bowls of *cozze* (mussels) and home-made pasta while housewives can be glimpsed through doorways hand-rolling *orecchiette* (ear-shaped pasta) or in the alleys or squares frying *sgagliozze* (squares of polenta). The Baresi love their sushi and at the fish market you can see them opening freshly caught sea urchins and mussels, sprinkling them with lemon juice and washing them down with a bottle of chilled Peroni.

On the western edge is the vast **Castello Normanno Svevo** Ⓐ (Norman Swabian Castle, Wed–Mon 8.30am–7.30pm). One of Frederick II's many fortifications, this was built in 1233–40 over the ruins of a Norman fortress, from which it retains two towers, later embellished and converted into a splendid dwelling by the Aragonese. To access the castle cross the bridge over the moat that is now a public garden. Unlike most Puglian castles there is a fair amount to see inside, including temporary exhibitions, archaeological remains, ceramics and the particularly appealing Gallery of Plaster Casts, exhibiting reproductions of medieval and post-medieval architectural features, including capitals, corbels and gargoyles, all from major monuments and museums in Puglia.

On Piazza dell'Odegitria you're unlikely to miss the **Cattedrale di San Sabino** Ⓑ (Mon–Sat 8am–12.30pm, 4–7.30pm, Sun 8am–12.30pm, 5–8.30pm). The majestic white facade, with a soaring bell-tower, dominates the square and looks particularly stunning against a blue sky. The church was dedicated to St Sabinus, a bishop of Canosa, whose remains were brought here in the 9th century, and which today lie in the crypt. The church was transformed from its Baroque excess to the simple style of the original Puglian-Romanesque. Below the cathedral the **Museo del Succorpo della Cattedrale** (Mon–Wed, Sat–Sun 9.30am–4pm, Thurs and Fri 9.30am–12.30pm) is a hidden gem, retaining the remains of earlier buildings, including a medieval Christian basilica on the same site. On show are some remarkable mosaics, tombs and part of a Roman road – all with good explanations in English.

North of the cathedral in the heart of old Bari rises the austere, almost fortress-like **Basilica di San Nicola** C (Mon–Sat 7.30am–7.30pm, Sun 7.30am–10pm), one of the first great Norman churches in Southern Italy. In 1087, 62 sailors from Bari left for Myra in Lycia (present-day Turkey) and purloined the relics of bishop Nicholas. A Byzantine edifice in Bari was transformed into a magnificent basilica, construction of which lasted for over a century, and the saint's relics were housed in the beautiful crypt – where they still lie. For centuries the basilica has been a destination for pilgrims from all over the Christian world who come to see the shrine containing the remains. San Nicola has always overshadowed the city's cathedral since at the time of construction the importance of a town was determined by the relics it held, gained at any cost and by any means. Within the enclosure of the San Nicola Citadel lies the pretty Romanesque **Chiesa di San Gregorio** D, the oldest consecrated church in Bari, dating back to the 10th century. North of San Nicola lies the newly-reopened **Museo Archeologico di Santa Scolastica** E (www.beniculturalionline.it/location-3819Museo-Archeologico-di-Santa-Scolastica.php; Mon, Wed–Sat 10am–5pm, Sun 10am–2pm). Set in the ancient monastery of Santa Scolastica the museum is incorporated within a 16th century bastion, the gateway to Old Bari for those arriving at the city by sea. A modern museum, with a multimedia route, it has beautifully arranged exhibits from Puglian prehistory to the Bronze Age, along with jewellery and other treasures from the Greek, Byzantine and medieval periods.

In the evenings life focuses on **Piazza Mercantile** F , a handsome square fringed by open-air restaurants and overlooked by the Palazzo del Sedile and the Colonna della Giustizia (Column of Justice) where debtors were exposed to public ridicule. The adjoining Piazza del Ferrarese is home to the tourist office.

POLIGNANO A MARE

A favourite excursion for the Baresi is the photogenic and fashionable resort of **Polignano a Mare** 18, 34km (21 miles) south of the city. The town perches high on the cliffs above the waters of the

Polignano a Mare, a cliff-diver's paradise

Adriatic – so high in fact that the resort is now a venue for the Red Bull Cliff Diving World Series, whose elite cliff-divers compete from heights of up to 27m (89ft) in chosen places around the globe. Once a year the cliff-divers gather here, accessing platforms up to this height through a private house in the cliffs. Around 70,000 fans flock to Polignano to watch the event while at other times of the year adrenalin junkies enjoy jumping into the water from the top of the rocks.

Twenty years ago Polignano a Mare was almost derelict, a coastal town in a poor agricultural region. Now it is one of the best-known spots on the Adriatic: a thriving resort with 85,000 annual visitors, a lively restaurant and bar scene, spectacular boat trips along the cave-riddled cliffs and entertaining rickshaw rides with food and wine tasting. The historic centre, built on the clifftops,

Ruins at Egnazia

POLIGNANO A MARE

is small but appealing with its little whitewashed alleys, narrow flights of steps and terraces with stunning views of the sea and coastline. When the wind is up, this is a popular spot to watch the waves crash against the cliffs. Just below the old town lies Cala Porto, a cove flanked by cliffs where the sea is crystal clear. It's ideal out of season but there's not a spare inch on the pebble beach in July and August.

> ### Volare…oh, oh!
>
> If you're a fan of the famous Italian song *'Volare'* don't miss the statue of its singer, Domenico Modugno, Polignano's favourite son. He stands with arms outstretched on the seafront just west of Cala Porto. He enjoyed jumping from the nearby cliffs into the sea – which is said to have inspired *'Volare'* (to fly).

A walk west along the cliffs will bring you to the **Fondazione Museo Pino Pascali** (www.museopinopascali.it; Wed–Sat 4–8pm), a striking museum of contemporary art in a converted abattoir overlooking the sea. The museum was officially opened in 2012 and displays works by artist, sculptor and set-designer, Pino Pascali (1935–68) who was born in Bari and lived for some time in Polignano a Mare. He died tragically in a motorbike accident in Rome at the age of 33. The museum also exhibits contemporary works by other Puglian artists and hosts temporary exhibitions, events, seminars and workshops.

A short drive along the coast brings you to the city of **Monopoli** [19], with a large, lavish cathedral, a seafront castle, a fishing port and good beaches. **Egnazia** [20], 18km (11 miles) to the south, was the site of a fourth-century Greco-Roman or Greco-Massapian town, and preserves ruins of foundations of houses, roads and tombs. It's a pretty setting by the sea but you need a good imagination to envisage this one-time key settlement on the Via Appia.

For most tourists the area is best known for the *de luxe* Borgo Egnazia (see page 136) where Justin Timberlake and Jessica Biel tied the knot in 2012.

VALLE D'ITRIA

Spreading over the provinces of Bari, Brindisi and Taranto, the Valle d'Itria is best known for the white cities that crown its hilltops and for the distinctive dwellings known as *trulli*. These small, conical-roofed, whitewashed houses have dotted the landscape for centuries. The town of Alberobello, a UNESCO World Heritage site, has them en masse, but you can also see them in their natural surroundings, among the vines, olives and almonds, on the fertile plain between Locorotondo and Martina Franca. Fans of these

The weird and wonderful Grotte di Castellana

hobbit-style houses can stay in a *trullo* hotel – or pray in a *trullo* church. There is also the option of staying in one of the region's many *masserie,* the fortified farmhouses, many of which have been converted into boutique hotels or spa resorts.

GROTTE DI CASTELLANA

In 1938 a 3km (2 mile)-long labyrinth of underground caves and chambers was discovered 65m (213ft) below ground level near the town of Castellana, north of Alberobello. The **Grotte di Castellana** ㉑ (Piazzale Anelli; tel: 080 499 8221; 9am–6pm, shorter hours off season; tickets available at www.grottedicastellana.it, see website for tour times), often cited as the most spectacular caves in Italy, have remarkable stalactite and stalagmites, and weird and wonderful rock formations such as the Cyclops, Capitoline She-Wolf, Pillars of Hercules, Cathedral of Milan and Tower of Pisa. The chambers are reached by lift and visited either on a 1km (0.5 mile) 50-minute tour or the more spectacular two-hour 3km (2 mile) tour which includes the staggeringly beautiful **Grotta Bianca**, an alabaster cavern with cream-coloured, needle-sharp stalactites. The temperature is around 18°C (64°F) all year so you may need an extra layer of clothing – as well as comfortable shoes. On Speleonight Tours you can listen to the night sounds of the caves and watch the creepy crawlies that populate them. From April to December the biggest of the caves is the setting of the underground theatrical show, *Hell in the Cave,* inspired by Dante's Inferno.

ALBEROBELLO

Few places in Puglia have better signage than **Alberobello** ㉒, where tourists flock to see the fairy-tale forest of *trulli*. The old part of town has around 1,500 of these quaint, beehive-shaped buildings. Brown signs lead you to the well-worn **Rione Monti** street in the upper part of town, flanked by shops selling mini *trulli*, olive oil, crafts and multi-coloured creamy liqueurs. *Trulli* owners will invite you in for free tasting of local products. The street climbs up to the Church of Sant'Antonio, also a *trullo* but a relatively modern one, dating from 1927. The less touristy and more tranquil part of the Trulli Zone is the **Rione Aia Piccola** quarter on the eastern side. Many of the dwellings here are family homes and not given over to tourism. The only two-storey *trullo* is the **Trullo Sovrano** (Piazza Sacramento 10; 10am–6pm, off-season 10am–12.45pm, 3.30–6pm) on the northern edge of town, now a museum, furnished as it would have been when occupied in the 18th century.

LOCOROTONDO

One of the most picturesque towns of Puglia, **Locorotondo** ㉓ (Round Place) takes its name from the setting. Less well-known

TRULLI EXTRAORDINARY

Some sources maintain that the original *trulli* were built by Byzantine monks as early as the 8th century, others that they were primitive tombs and that the various symbols on the roofs have magic, Christian or pagan significance. However, some experts think the explanation is more simple – they were built from the early 16th century by shepherds and farmers with stones cleared from the fields. There is also a theory that the ancient building style was revived to thwart the tax collectors of the Kingdom of the Two Sicilies: the dwellings had dry stone walls so could be dismantled quickly before the tax collector arrived – then later rebuilt. The oldest *trulli* still standing date from the 17th century. Out in the country you can find *trulli* (and *trulli*-inspired) farms, barns, grain silos and even petrol stations.

than nearby Alberobello, it is a white hilltop town laid out in concentric circles. The dazzling white houses and the vast dome and lofty bell-tower of the neoclassical Chiesa di San Giorgio can be seen from afar and from the town itself there are fine views out over the vineyards of the Itria Valley. The vines produce white, red and rosé wines but the town is best known for the white Locorotondo DOP.

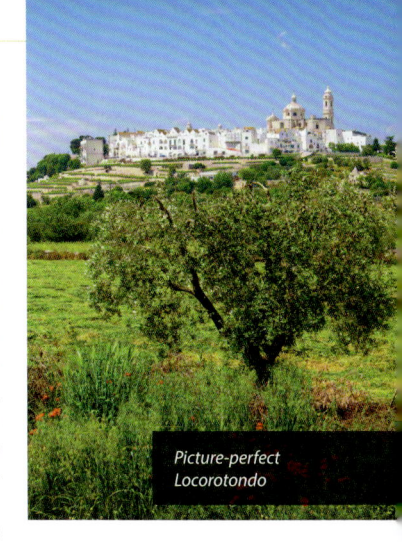

Picture-perfect Locorotondo

Once fortified with walls and keeps, the historical centre retains some fine palazzi and churches, quiet courtyards and winding cobbled alleys. Everything is daubed in dazzling whitewash, contrasting with the lush green of potted plants and brilliant reds of geraniums or hibiscus. It is a lovely spot for a stroll, and has some tempting little tavernas and places for *degustazione* (tasting) of the local specialities: *salumi*, cheeses, olive oil and *taralli* (round biscuits).

MARTINA FRANCA

The largest and liveliest town of the Valle d'Itria is **Martina Franca** ㉔, renowned for its Baroque architecture. The site was settled in the 10th century by fugitives from Taranto escaping Saracen invaders but was largely developed in the 14th century when Philip of Anjou granted it fiscal exemptions – hence the Franca (Free) part of the name (Martina comes from San Martino, the patron saint). The charm of the town lies in narrow streets, fine

Piazza Plebiscito, Martina Franca

churches and graceful 18th-century town houses, with Baroque features and beautiful wrought-iron balconies. The town is lively and civilised, known for its chic shops and gastronomy, based on superb cold meats (see box), cheeses and pasta. There is also a local white wine, Martina Franca, which comes either still or sparkling (*Spumante*).

The spacious tree-lined **Piazza XX Settembre**, the town's main square, is a popular rendezvous and the venue of the *passeggiata*. Heralding the old city is the triumphal arch known as the **Porto Santo Stefano** (also known as the Arco di Sant'Antonio). Just to the right of it is the tourist office which provides a free map, suggesting five walking itineraries and no less than 53 cultural attractions. Beyond the arch, overlooking the Piazza Roma and the Dolphin Fountain, you are unlikely to miss the grand **Palazzo Ducale** (Ducal Palace; Mon–Thurs 10am–1pm, 3–9pm, Fri–Sun 10am–1pm, 3–11pm; charge only for royal apartments). On the site of the 14th century Orsini castle, this 17th-century palace was built for the Caracciolo dukes who ruled here in the city's heyday. It is now the town hall but you can visit the royal apartments on the *piano nobile,* hung with Murano glass chandeliers and adorned with rococo murals (1776) by Domenico Carella. These depict the ducal family in scenes from Roman and Greek mythology and from the Bible.

The Corso Vittorio Emanuele, lined by chic shops, leads to **Piazza Plebiscito**, dwarfed by the lofty and undulating Baroque facade of the **Chiesa di San Martino**. A sculptural group over the main portal shows St Martin, the city's patron saint, swinging a sword and sharing his cloak with a beggar. The church has a richly adorned interior with a profusion of coloured marble. Beyond it, the Palazzo dell'Università with stone carvings is flanked by a baroque clock tower and in the next square a lovely Baroque *portico* shelters a couple of the city's many restaurants. At the end of

CAPOCOLLO DI MARTINA FRANCA

Carnivores shouldn't miss out on Capocollo di Martina Franca, a speciality of the region since the 18th century. This sweet, delicately smoked, cured ham was awarded 'Slow Food' protected status. The pork, which comes from prized pigs of the Murgia region, is rubbed with salt, pepper and spices and left for 15 days. After being marinated in herbs and *Vin Cotto* (a 'cooked' wine, slowly simmered until thick and syrupy), it is stuffed into a natural casing and left for about a fortnight. It is then smoked with the bark of oak, almond husks and Mediterranean herbs and left to cure for at least three months. The meat is often served with other salamis from the region or as a filler for *panini* with Pecorino or Canestrato cheese. A bottle of Primitivo wine is the perfect accompaniment.

A snapshot of trulli heaven

Via Garibaldi brown signs point you left and right in the direction of nine monuments, taking you along winding narrow alleys to the edge of the walled city.

CISTERNINO

On the edge of the Valle d'Istria, **Cisternino** ❷⑤ is a delightful little town of whitewashed houses perched on a hilltop and surrounded by olive groves. The old quarter has a typically Asian look with houses built around an inner courtyard with outer staircases leading to the upper floors. The town has more than its fair share of family-run, simple trattorias, many of them meat-focused. The town is known as *la città della bombetta*, the *bombetta* being parcels of meat, usually thin slices of pork (or other meat) filled with cheese or more meat and spices, then rolled up and cooked on a grill or in the oven (or taken home to cook). Accompaniments such as bread and wine are usually on hand.

OSTUNI

The best known of the region's *'città bianche'* (white cities), **Ostuni** ❷⓿ stretches dramatically over three hilltops, overlooking plains of olive groves. The historic centre, surrounded by city walls, has steep winding alleys, fine Baroque buildings and a jumbled pyramid of chalk-white, flat-roofed houses.

The focus of town life is the **Piazza della Libertà**, overlooked by the stately Municipio (Town Hall) and the **Chiesa di San Francesco** which at first glance looks Renaisssance but was almost entirely rebuilt. The marble statues of St Francis of Assisi and St Anthony of Padua in the niches on the facade for example are 20th century. At the far end a 20m (65ft) decorative **Obelisco di Sant'Oronzo** is topped by a statue of the city's patron saint, Sant'Oronzo. He was credited with ending the plague in the city in 1656 and every year is honoured with a three-day festival in Ostuni (25–27 August). From Piazza della Libertà the cobbled Via Cattedrale climbs up towards the historic centre, and is flanked by shops selling local crafts and gastronomic delights. En route stop at the **Museo Civico**, which is also known as the Museo di Civiltà Preclassiche della Murgia Meridionale (Museum of Preclassical Civilisation of Southern Murgia; www.ostunimuseo.it/museo-civico; Mon–Fri 10am–6pm, Sat–Sun 10am–7pm) within the mid-18th-century Church of San Vito Martire (known as Le Monacelle). The most famous of its archaeological exhibits that exists is a 27,000 year-old skeleton of a young woman known as Delia which was discovered in 1991 in a grotto close to Ostuni. It was surrounded by the skeletons and teeth of animals which would have been hunted by her tribe. But the most remarkable discovery was the fact that she was pregnant and bore the skeleton of the dead foetus in her womb. The remains were carefully removed from the cave and they were taken for safekeeping to Ostuni's museum.

At the heart of Ostuni's old quarter and dominating the tallest hill is the late Gothic **Cattedrale** (1435–95). It has an elegant and unusual facade, with its pointy top, curves and magnificent rose window, decorated with zoomorphical and biblical scenes. The Latin-cross interior was completely remodelled in the 18th century, with Baroque chapels on the sides. The Palazzo Vescovile (Bishop's Palace) and the Palazzo del Seminario, with an arched loggia connecting the two, look on to the same square as the church, creating a theatre-stage effect. The narrow streets beyond, with Baroque portals, *palazzi* and small squares, are well worth exploring.

Ostuni's old quarter

THE SALENTO

The Salentine Peninsula or Salento is framed by the Ionian and Adriatic Seas and stretches to the most southerly part of Italy's heel. It is famed for its sun-baked beaches and sees relatively few tourists outside the high season. But Salento also has plenty of cultural interest, embracing the beautiful Baroque city of Lecce, the lovely coastal towns of Otranto and Gallipoli, the 'Greek' towns south of Lecce as well as sleepy southern villages. Life is relaxed and slow-paced here. Nothing is contrived or picture perfect – which of course is all part of its charm.

BRINDISI

Historic **Brindisi** ❷ has been a busy port since ancient times. In Roman times it was the most important port in southern Italy, and was linked to Rome by the 350 mile (563km)-long Appian Way (Via Antica) which facilitated trade and travel to Greece and the east. Today Brindisi teems with travellers throughout the summer, most en route to Greece. It is not a city where many tourists choose to stay but it has a handful of historic sights, and the seafront with its palms and white canopied cafés is a pleasant place to stroll. Across the harbour rises the **Monumento Al Marinaio d'Italia** (Monument to Italian Sailors; Thurs–Tues 10am–6pm; free), a soaring, rudder-shaped tower in memory of fallen soldiers between Unification and 1933 – the date of the monument. It is built in typical fascist style and has panoramic views of the city and harbour from the top.

Waterfront restaurant in Brindisi

From the waterfront a sweeping flight of steps, known as the **Scalinata Virgiliana**, ascends to the **Roman Column**, marking the terminus of the Via Appia. One of the two columns collapsed in 1528 and was taken to Lecce where it now supports a bronze statue of the city's patron saint, St Oronzo. As you look at the column with your back to the sea, the slightly derelict house to your left with a modern ground floor is, according to some historians, the house where Virgil spent the last days of his life.

An archway leads to the **Duomo** (Cathedral) where Frederick II married his second wife Yolande in 1225. The church was destroyed by an earthquake in 1743 and rebuilt. The nearby **Museo Archeologico Provinciale Ribezzo** (Tues–Sun 9.30am–7.30pm) has three floors of archaeological treasures, from fine Attic ceramics to an exceptional collection of Hellenistic bronzes which

Brindisi's Duomo

were discovered at the bottom of the sea near Brindisi harbour in the early 1990s.

The tourist office is located on Via Duomo in the beautiful **Palazzo Granafei-Nervegna**, part of which houses the huge capital that topped one of the Roman Columns. It is kept here to preserve it from sea-salt erosion (the one on the column is a copy). At this level you can appreciate all the detail including tritons and male and female sea-gods. West of the palace the **Tempio di San Giovanni al Sepolcro** (Tues–Sun 8am–8.30pm; free) on the eponymous piazza is a gem of a church, constructed on the lines of the Holy Sepulchre in Jerusalem. It was built at the behest of Norman prince Bohemond who wanted to show his gratitude for the success of the First Crusade, of which he had been one of the leaders. It has a fine Norman portal and a lovely, intimate interior with 13th–15th century frescoes.

LECCE

Lecce 28 was once a key crossroads of the Mediterranean, coveted by foreign invaders over the centuries. Today it's best known as the Baroque gem of Puglia. The exuberant decorative style known as 'Lecce Baroque' began in the mid-17th century and flourished for about 60 years. In a land of stout Norman castles and restrained Romanesque churches, the city of fanciful facades at every turn comes as a glorious surprise. Aided by the softness of the local limestone, the stonemasons let their chisels run wild. Balconies are supported by grinning caryatids, classical columns are festooned with foliage, window frames are laden with swags of fruit while portals drip with trophies and crests. The main architect was Giuseppe Zimbalo, familiarly known as 'Lo Zingarello', the Little Gypsy. The city has over 40 churches (along with countless Baroque palazzi and a castle), of which only the main ones in the centre are covered below.

> **Baroque pasta**
>
> After a day taking in Lecce's lavish architecture, you might like to try a very apt local speciality: *sagne n'cannulate*. This pasta dish, traditionally served with a simple tomato and cheese sauce, is made with long twisted ribbons of pasta which mimic the city's swirling architecture.

Lecce is also a university town, with a lively cultural programme and some excellent restaurants. It is known for its cuisine and cookery schools where you can learn how to make local pasta from scratch and visit markets and food and wine producers.

Piazza Sant'Oronzo

In the heart of Lecce is **Piazza Sant'Oronzo**, whose history spans 2,000 years. St Oronzo, the city's patron saint, blesses the city from atop the soaring Roman column which was donated by Brindisians in the belief that Oronzo had saved their city from the plague. Below lie the remains of a **Roman Amphitheatre** dating from the 2nd century AD and seating around 25,000. It was only rediscovered during works in the early 20th century when a large part of the piazza was destroyed for the construction of the Banca d'Italia. Mussolini resurrected the theatre ruins (the upper level was lost though the pillars still stand) but also added fascist architecture resulting in the hotchpotch of styles in the square you see today. The amphitheatre was opened in 2000 as a concert venue after a six-year restoration but is now roped off (but visible) to prevent any further deterioration. Finds from the amphitheatre can be seen at the city's archaeological museum, the Museo Provinciale Sigismondo Castromediano, Viale Gallipoli, 28 (Tues–Sun 4–8pm; free). The unusual Renaissance pavilion or **Sedile** on the Piazza Sant'Oronzo has variously served as the seat of the mayor, the Town Council, the National Guard and the municipal museum.

Much of it was demolished by Mussolini and today it houses the tourist information office (conveniently open daily until 9pm).

Basilica di Santa Croce

The most complete expression of Leccese Baroque is the **Basilica di Santa Croce** (Via Umberto I; daily 9am–9pm) just to the north of Piazza Sant'Oronzo. The medieval cathedral which formerly stood here was demolished and rebuilt by Zimbalo. Looking at the wildly elaborate facade, with its large and lavish rose window and profusion of *putti*, strange beasts, sea gods and caryatids, it comes as no surprise to learn that the church took nearly 150 years to build (1549–1695). The interior, where the predominant style is late Renaissance, is restrained in comparison to the facade. Zimbalo also built the adjoining Baroque Convento dei

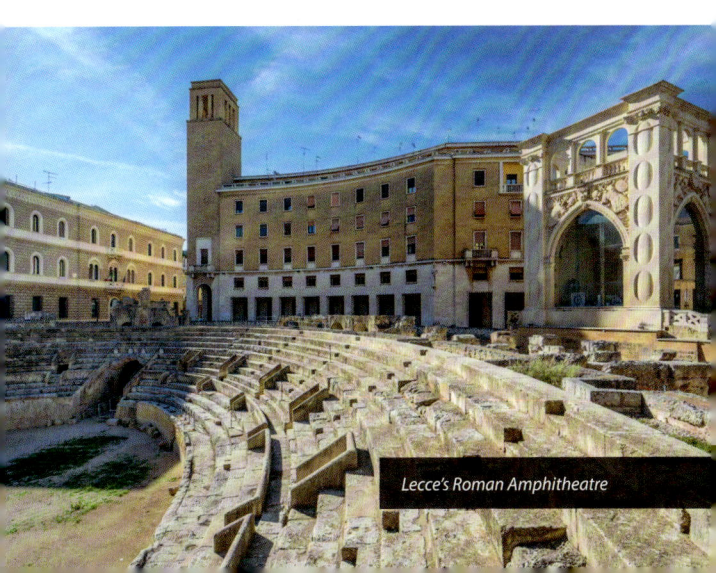

Lecce's Roman Amphitheatre

In the streets of Lecce

Celestini, now the Palazzo della Provincia, occupied by Government offices. Just south of the Basilica on the site of the old synagogue is the Museo Ebraico (Jewish Museum, Via Umberto 1, No 9, www.palazzotaurino.com; Mon–Sat 10am–5pm, Sun 10.30am–1.30pm) focuses on the once thriving Jewish community in medieval Lecce.

Piazza del Duomo

Lecce's stunning **Piazza del Duomo**, west of Piazza Sant'Otranzo, is a triumph of Lecce Baroque, at its most theatrical at night when floodlit. This has always been a stage set for lavish religious and civic celebrations and today is the setting in summer for concerts and ballets. The piazza is framed by the facades of the Duomo, the Palazzo Vescovile (Episcopal Palace) and the Seminario (Seminary), all built or reworked in the 17th century. Unusually the **Duomo** has two facades: the theatrical one facing the opening to the piazza, conceived as a triumphal arch, and the more austere, older facade at the eastern end. The lofty campanile, built separately from the Duomo, formerly served as a watchtower. Today there is no public access – unless you are Madonna, who was allowed to climb to the top in 2017. Inside the Duomo, the riot of multi-coloured marble, gilt stucco and statues is typical of the ornate local style.

Overlooking the Piazzetta Vittorio Emanuele II, east of the Duomo, the **Chiesa di Santa Chiara** has a highly decorative facade and ornate altar as well as some remarkable examples of papier-mâché (*cartapestra*). Look up at the ceiling – you would never know it wasn't wood. The art dates back to the 17th century and most of the Lecce churches feature at least one *cartapestra* statue. There are still workshops in the city where you can buy finely crafted pieces.

Zimbalo is buried in the **Basilica di San Giovanni Battista** therwise known as the Basilica **del Rosario** (Via Giuseppe Libertini 5, in the southwest corner of town; 8.30–11.30am, 4.30–6pm; free). The exuberant facade is only rivalled by that of Lecce's Santa Croce.

Abbazia di Santa Maria di Cerrate

In a country setting amongst olive groves, 20 minutes' drive north of Lecce, lies the lovely Romanesque **Abbazia di Santa Maria di Cerrate** (www.fondoambiente.it/

MUSEO ARCHEOLOGICO FAGGIANO

In 2001 Luciano Faggiano purchased a building on Via Ascanio Grandi in Lecce with the intention of creating a trattoria. The toilet was malfunctioning so he and his two elder sons dug down to find a sewage pipe. On the way they discovered 2,000 years of history. Archaeological finds on various levels of the foundations included a Messapian tomb, a Roman granary, etchings from the Knights Templar and remains from a Franciscan Convent. The trattoria was never built, digging went on for years and the building became a museum in 2008: the **Museo Archeologico Faggiano** (www.museofaggiano.it; daily 9.30am–8pm). Around 4,000 archaeological artefacts were discovered, many of which are stored under Lecce's castle, others in the museum.

Abbazia di Santa Maria di Cerrate

abbazia-di-santa-maria-di-cerrate-eng; on SP100; Tues–Sun March, April, May, Sept and Oct 10am–6pm, Nov–Dec 10am–4pm; June–Aug daily 9.30am–1pm, 3.30–7.30pm). This ex-Greek Orthodox monastery was once a cultural hub of southern Italy which later expanded into farming. The site was sacked by Turkish pirates in 1711 and left abandoned. In 2012 it was entrusted to the FAI, (Fondo Ambiente Italiano), the Italian National Trust, for major restoration and has recently opened to the public.

THE GRECIA SALENTINA

South of Lecce lies the area known as Grecia Salentina, an area of Greek colonisation where you can still very occasionally hear the older generation speak *griko*, a Greek dialect. The first settlers arrived in the 8th century, fleeing from religious persecution in Greece. They founded monasteries, set up communities and began the wine and olive oil industries. By the 10th century there were around 40 villages whose language, clothing, food and habits were entirely Greek. The Norman invasion in the early 11th century saw the start of the decline of the villages, but there are still religious buildings dating from its Greek heyday, flat houses which look more Greek than Italian and signs in Greek as well as Italian. One of the remaining ten or so Greek villages is **Calimera** (Kalimera in Greek means 'good morning'), another is **Corigliano d'Otranto** ㉙ a former centre of Greek language and culture, with a dominant castle and a market where you might just catch a phrase or two of *griko*.

OLIVE TREES IN PERIL

Puglia is renowned for olive trees, some of them centuries old. Until recently it produced around 40 percent of the olive oil exported from Italy. But in 2013 Salento was hit by a vicious bacterium, *Xyella fastidiosa*, believed to have arrived in Italy on exotic plants from Costa Rica. The cause is a tiny pest called the spittlebug. The result has been the desiccation of olive groves and the loss or threatened loss of business to families who have been producing olive oil for generations. Around a third of Puglia's olive trees have been affected and the disease is advancing north. In an effort to eradicate the spread an EU commission stipulated that farmers uproot infected trees and in some cases destroy other olive trees, however healthy, within 100 metres (109 yards) of the ones affected. There is no known cure but the felling of so many trees is hotly disputed, not just by farmers but by bacteria experts and plant pathologists who believe that the bacterium can be treated with natural remedies. Meanwhile the race is on to discover olive cultivars resistant to the disease which could replace the dead trees.

The Grecia Salentina hosts one of Europe's most important music festivals, dedicated to traditional culture: **La Notte della Taranta** (www.lanottedellataranta.it/en). The festival is dedicated to the rediscovery of Salento's folk music and its fusion with other genres of music, be it rock, jazz or classical. Every August over 200,000 spectators flock to the region to hear concerts in the villages, the grand finale being the famous Concertone, held at Melpignano. Each year the taranta folk dance is performed at the Festival of SS Pietro e Paolo (28–30 June) in the eponymous church at the town of **Galatina** ㉚ on the edge of the Grecia Salentina. The main monument of this quite smart, ex-Greek city is the beautiful late Romanesque Basilica of Santa Caterina d'Alessandria whose walls are embellished with remarkable 14th-century frescoes depicting biblical scenes.

OTRANTO

South-east of Lecce, **Otranto** ㉛ is Italy's most easterly town, built on a rocky promontory and facing the shores of Albania. A town of Greek origin, it became the main port on the eastern coast of the Adriatic. The location made it vulnerable to attacks, the most notorious of which was the 1480 siege by an Ottoman fleet carrying 18,000 troops. The Otranto people refused to surrender. Thousands were killed,

The mosaicked floor inside Otranto Cathedral

including all males over 15, and 5,000 were enslaved. Some 800 survivors were offered mercy if they embraced the Muslim faith. They refused and were all beheaded, along with their executioner who was so impressed by their steadfastness that he announced an untimely conversion to the Christian faith. The Chiesa dei Martiri (Church of the Martyrs) on the Hill of Minerva just up from the centre, marks the spot where the 800 were beheaded. They were canonised by Pope Francis in 2013 and are known as the Blessed Martyrs of Otranto.

Castello and Cattedrale

Otranto's picturesque historic quarter, seafront restaurants and fine white beaches combine to make it one of Puglia's most sought-after resorts. (Steer clear in high season when it's teeming.) The old centre, on a hill, is heralded by the **Castello Aragonese** (10am–midnight summer, 10am–6pm off season), built by Ferdinand of Aragon in the late 15th century, following the Ottoman invasion of 1480. Many English who visit Otranto associate the town with Horace Walpole who wrote the novel *The Castle of Otranto* (1764), generally regarded as the first Gothic novel. In fact the only reason he chose the title was because he liked the 'sonorous name' – he never actually went there.

But Otranto's star sight is the **Cattedrale dell'Annunziata** (June–Sept 7am–noon, 3–8pm, Oct–May closes 5pm) on Piazza Duomo, built by the Normans in the 11th century. This church retains a stunning rose window and an even more stunning mosaic, covering the entire floor of the basilica. It represents *The Tree of Life*, whose branches bear naive depictions of the Labours of the Month (showing the relevant agricultural or domestic activity) and scenes from the Bible and mythology. In the right isle of the church the gruesome **Capella dei Martiri** displays behind glass panels the bones of the martyrs slain by the Saracens. Otranto's first cathedral was the **Basilica di San Pietro** on Via San Pietro, in the oldest part of the town, a jewel of a church dating back to the 9th century with a Greek-cross plan and faded frescoes.

Otranto has long stretches of sandy beaches to the north of the town, backed by pine forests and lapped by the limpid, blue-green sea. One of the most sought-after beaches is the **Baia dei Turchi** ㉜, packed in high season when it is linked to Otranto by shuttle bus.

SOUTH FROM OTRANTO

Once you have reached Otranto it is hard to resist the temptation to visit Italy's Land's End at Santa Maria di Leuca. A wild and rocky shoreline, characterised by spits of land jutting into the sparkling seas and ruined watchtowers, gives way to a dramatic corniche

Baia dei Turchi, popular for a reason

SANTA MARIA DI LEUCA

running through small resorts. On a clear day, if you strain your eyes, you might just spot the coast of Corfu and southern Albania. The drive is not recommended in high season when traffic can be nose-to-tail.

Castro

Roughly half way between Otranto and Santa Maria de Leuca is the appealing town of **Castro** ㉝, overlooking the sea. It dates back to pre-Roman times, has a fine Aragonese castle, built on foundations of earlier fortresses, a charming old town with a Romanesque cathedral and a rocky coast riddled with caves. Spectacular sea views can be enjoyed from the panoramic piazza above the port. The most famous of its caves is the seductively named **La Grotta Zinzulusa** ㉞ (daily summer 9.30am–6.30pm, off-season 10.30am–4.30pm, guided tours only, accessible by boat and road), named after the stalactites that resemble dangling strips of cloth ('*zinzuli*' in local dialect). This is a highly popular tourist attraction although the caves are not as beautiful as those of Castellana (see page 53).

Porto Badisco

Just over 10km (6 miles) south of Otranto lies a delightful secluded bay called Porto Badisco. Virgil cites it as the spot where Aeneas first stepped foot onto Italian shores after his escape from Troy. The crystalline waters are perfect for swimming, snorkelling and diving. In the rocks just to the north lies the Grotta dei Cervi (Cave of the Deer) with traces of prehistoric cave paintings including depictions of deer.

SANTA MARIA DI LEUCA

The resort town of **Santa Maria di Leuca** ㉟ lies at the end of the road, on the southern tip of Italy, where the Ionian and Adriatic

Santa Maria di Leuca

seas meet. A sign in the piazza informs you that this is *Finibus Terrae*, the end of the earth as the Romans called it. Near the lighthouse on the windswept rocky promontory a column erected by Mussolini marks the terminus of the Apulian Aqueduct (see box). On the rare occasions when there is an excess of water the floodgates are opened, creating a monumental cascade of water into the sea. At the top of the hill near the lighthouse and overlooking the sea, the **Basilica Santuario di Santa Maria de Finibus Terrae** is a place of pilgrimage constructed over the ruins of a pagan temple to Minerva and rebuilt many times after attacks by Moorish corsairs.

GALLIPOLI

Watchtowers dot the Ionian coastline between Santa Maria di Leuca and Gallipoli, with resorts and beaches in between. The 8km (5 mile) stretch of fine white sands and shallow crystalline water at **Marina di Pescoluse**, at the southern end, is known as the Maldives of Salento.

The historic port of **Gallipoli** ❸⓺ may not quite live up to its name (*Kalos Polis* means 'beautiful city' in Greek) but it certainly has plenty of charm and is well worth visiting for the old walled town, fishing port, churches, nearby beaches and delicious seafood dishes. The historic centre is set on an island which is joined to the new town by a bridge (in summer you have to park on the mainland and walk across). The prominent **Castello Angioino** (Tues–Sun 10am–6pm, 5pm off season), heralding the historic centre, was built by the Aragonese and remodelled in the 17th

THE GREAT APULIAN AQUEDUCT

Man-made aqueducts in parched areas of Europe have existed since the 6th century BC when the ancient Greeks constructed the Eupalinian Aqueduct to supply Samos. But few people have heard of the 'The Great Aqueduct of Apulia', one of the most impressive hydraulic engineering systems in the world for size and capacity. Until World War I Puglia was seriously arid, bedevilled by poor farming conditions and poverty. There were no useful rivers to channel, so in the early 20th century civil engineers tapped the water from the Sele River in the mountains in Campania on the western slope of the Apennine watershed. The first section, bringing water to Bari, was functioning by 1915 and the entire aqueduct was inaugurated in 1939 under Mussolini as part of his ambitious building programme. Today it stretches for 2,189km (1,360 miles), terminating at Santa Maria di Leuca, and serves four million Pugliesi in 258 cities, towns and villages. The solution of such a fundamental natural problem afflicting such a large region by a single engineering feat makes this aqueduct notable if not unique.

century. Today it is a cultural centre, hosting temporary exhibitions and concerts. Below the bridge, the **fish market** is one of the liveliest in Puglia, with a huge range of fish and seafood. Come for *Aperfish*, an early evening fish snack (Mon–Fri) with an *aperitivo* and look out for *gamberoni viola* (purple prawns) *di Gallipoli*, a local speciality. The centre of the old town has handsome Spanish-style palazzi with courtyards, carvings and wrought-iron balconies. On one of the narrow cobbled alleyways is the Baroque **Cattedrale di Sant'Agata**, with its rich, honey-coloured facade. Nearby the **Frantoio Ipogeo** is one of many underground tufa caves where olive oil used to be pressed – the city was a major exporter of olive oil in its heyday. A stroll around the **bastions** affords fine sea views, tavernas with terraces and some delightful Baroque churches.

Gallipoli harbour and castle

TARANTO

Founded by Spartan colonisers in 706BC, ancient **Taras (Taranto)** ㊲ was in the 4th century BC the largest city in Magna Graecia, boasting a population of 300,000 and a city wall 15km (9 miles) in circumference. It became a thriving commercial seaport, a hub of art and culture and, like many communities throughout Magna Graecia, a centre of Pythagorean philosophy. All that remains of this era in Taranto are two columns of what was one of the most important Doric temples in Magna Graecia, dedicated to the god Poseidon.

> **Gallipoli's olive oil**
>
> In the 16th and 17th centuries Gallipoli was a prosperous city, exporting its renowned olive oil to many European capitals. This famous nectar was not used for drizzling on bread or salad but as fuel for the lamps in the city streets.

The steelworks and huge cranes as you approach Taranto don't endear you to the city and the old town on a small island is notoriously dark, dingy and run-down (watch your valuables and avoid going off the beaten track). In comparison the new 18th and 19th century town, on the mainland, is quite elegant and is visited by sightseers for the city's outstanding archaeological museum.

MArTA (Museo Archeologico Nazionale di Taranto)

Most tourists give Taranto a wide berth but for anyone interested in ancient Taras it is worth a visit if only for the MArTA or **Museo Archeologico Nazionale di Taranto** (Via Cavour 10; www.museotaranto.beniculturali.it/en; Tues–Sat 8.30am–7.30pm, Sun 9am–1pm, 3.30–7.30pm, Mon 8.30am–7.30pm but for groups only (3–30 people); last admission two hours before closing time). In southern Italy it is rivalled only by Naples' Archaeological Museum for the splendour of its antiquities. Archaeological finds

Taranto's Doric Columns

and artefacts, numbering around 200,000, range from the Paleolithic era through to the early Middle Ages. The exhibits include Greek and Roman sculpture, a series of wonderful Roman floor mosaics, one of the most important collections of ancient ceramics in Italy and, perhaps most famous of all, a collection of gold artefacts including exquisite jewellery from Magna Graecia.

Old Town

The *centro storico* or old town, bounded by the Small and the Great Seas, and accessed over the Ponte Girevole from the mainland, is dominated by the splendid **Castello Aragonese** (www.castelloaragonesetaranto.com; open daily, free multilingual guided visits from 9am to 1am, roughly every two hours, shorter hours off season). The castle, with its four sturdy cylindrical towers, was built in the 15th century to defend the city against invading Turks. In the 18th century it was converted into a prison, then donated in 1887 to the Italian Navy who still occupy it and Italian officers in uniform will show you round. Opposite the castle is the Baroque **Palazzo di Città**, palace of the governor (closed to the public).

Across the square from the castle are the two remaining **Doric Columns** from the Greek Temple. A stroll along the waterfront will bring you to the cloistered **Convento Santa Chiara** and, turning right up Vico Santa Chiara, to the **Cattedrale di San**

Cataldo. This was redesigned in Baroque style in the 17th and 18th century, and is notable for the inlaid marble and frescoes in the **Cappellone di San Cataldo**. This chapel houses relics of Taranto's patron saint, San Cataldo, who was to become its archbishop. Via Duomo leads to the **Chiesa di San Domenico**, founded by Frederick II in 1223, and today showcases a blend of medieval and Baroque.

The workshops of Grottaglie

East of Taranto, on a small hill, the town of **Grottaglie** ❸ takes its name from the grottoes carved from the *tufo*. Artisans here have been producing hand-made ceramics since medieval times. There are around 50 workshops, many of them sited within the caves.

THE TARANTELLA

If you are lucky enough to coincide with one of Puglia's festivals you may well hear the hypnotic music of the taranta, named after Taranto. Folklore has it that in the 15th to 17th centuries women working in the fields were bitten by Lycosa tarantula spiders (not to be confused with what is commonly known as a tarantula today) and infected with 'tarantism', the only cure for which was believed to be a frenzied non-stop spinning dance. This became known as the tarantella. There is no evidence that these spider bites were poisonous but the story has been passed down through the generations. Today's tarantella is not the hysterical dance of yore and is nearly always performed by two women or a man and a woman. It is most commonly accompanied by a mandolin, guitar, accordion and tambourine and varies from region to region. The main taranta event in Puglia is the Notte della Taranta, which tours around Salento and culminates in Melpignano in August.

Head for the *quartiere delle ceramiche* (ceramics quarter) along Via E Crispi, to watch potters turning clay, painting and creating jugs, urns, pots, crockery, lamps and decorative figures. Prices and quality vary but it is not hard to find beautifully made pieces in colourful traditional designs. Avoid afternoons (1/1.30pm–4.30pm) when the workshops are closed and note that on Sundays only some are open. The Museo della Ceramica (www.museogrottaglie.it), displaying 400 pieces, charts the history of the local ceramics industry from the 14th to the 20th century.

AN EXCURSION TO MATERA

The city of **Matera** 39 is located in the region of Basilicata rather than Puglia but it is only just across the border and it's well worth

Grottaglie, famous for its ceramics since medieval times

adding an extra day or two to your stay in Puglia to explore this intriguing city. It is just under 70km (43 miles) from Bari. The journey takes 65 minutes by bus (or 75 minutes by shuttle bus from the airport), 1hr 45 minutes by train and 60–70 minutes by car. Parking is prohibited in the old city (though you can usually drop your luggage if you're staying overnight) and finding a parking place in the new town is notoriously difficult.

'CITY OF SHAME'

Designated a UNESCO World Heritage site in 1993 and the first southern Italian city to be recognised as European Capital of Culture (2019), this is a beguiling town of troglodyte dwellings, evocative cave churches, houses piled on top of each other and abandoned hovels – all gouged out of the limestone *tufo* over the ages. It is said to be the third oldest continuously inhabited city in the world, with some caves dating back to the Palaeolithic age. Up until the 1950s the honeycomb of houses and caves known as Sassi (rocks) were home to peasants who lived in appalling conditions with an average of six children, together with the animals, in a single room. The Italian government, embarrassed by the 'City of Shame', moved out (at times forcefully) 15,000 residents into new, more modern quarters from 1953–68. In the 1980s a number of intrepid Materani started to return. Now the Sassi are Basilicata's main tourist attraction, recognised by UNESCO as 'the most outstanding, intact example of a troglodyte settlement in the Mediterranean region'.

SEEING THE CITY

A ridge, crowned by Matera's cathedral, splits the Sassi into two: the Sasso Barisano and the Sasso Caveoso. Both are a labyrinth of alleys, stone stairways and tiny courtyards. The best way to explore them is on foot, stopping perhaps at bars or restaurants to see the

Beguiling Matera

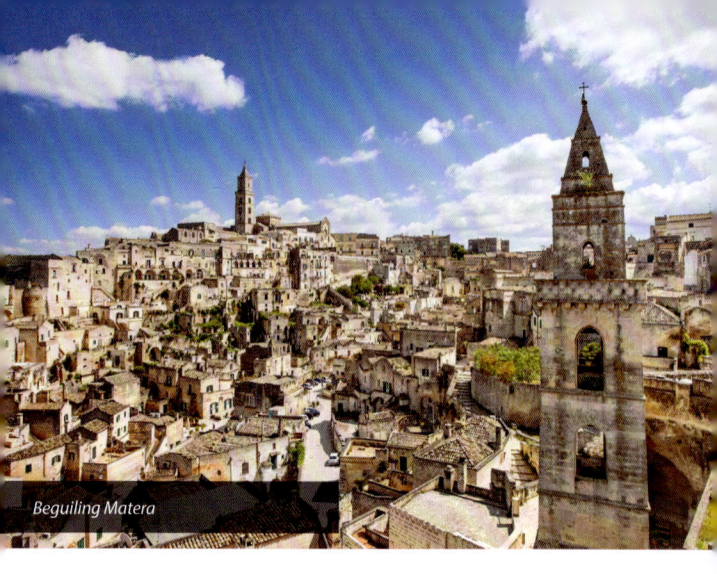

clever conversions from the original cave dwellings. But even with a map, GPS or the brown itinerary signs it's easy to get lost in the warren of multilayered alleys. Many visitors opt for a guided tour (arranged by the tourist office or one of the agencies). These are usually good value, informative and give access to Sassi which are otherwise inaccessible. Alternatively the tourist office provides a map of Matera with suggested itineraries.

The more interesting church interiors are those of the so-called *chiese rupestre*: the primitive churches carved into the hillsides by monks in the 9th to the 15th centuries. There are around 150 of these churches, with some 48 in the *Sassi* themselves, some preserving remarkable frescoes which you can admire to the sounds of background music (anything from Gregorian chants to *The Sound of Silence*). Most churches are open daily from 10am–7pm, Nov–March 10am–4pm. There is a charge for the rupestrian churches but cumulative tickets are available.

THE SASSI

You could spend several days exploring all the churches but if time is limited concentrate on the following half dozen. In the **Sasso Barisano** the highlights are the **Chiesa San Pietro Barisano**, with 15th- and 16th-century frescoes and burial niches where corpses were placed so that bodily fluids could drain into the porous rock, and the remarkable monastic complex of the **Chiesa di Madonna delle Virtù** and the **Chiesa di San Nicola dei Greci** above it, with glowing frescoes on the walls.

In the **Sasso Caveoso** it is worth seeking out the frescoed **Chiesa Santa Maria de Idris**, carved into the Idris rock and leading into the older and very evocative cave church of **San Giovanni in Monterrone**. The nearby basilica-style **Chiesa di Santa Lucia alle Malve** preserves some of its 11th–17th century frescoes, the most

Chiesa Santa Maria de Idris

AN EXCURSION TO MATERA

> ### Staying in the Sassi
>
> Matera has some very atmospheric accommodation in converted caves and it's well worth seeing the city in the evening, when the crowds have gone and the buildings are bathed in a golden light.

famous of which depicts a breastfeeding Madonna.

For an insight into bygone life you can visit caves which have been left more or less untouched since they were inhabited in the 1940s. Guides will tell you how cave-dwellers eked out a living, what they ate, how they washed and cooked and their ingenious systems to gather water from roofs, houses and streets. The **Casa-Grotta di Vico Solitario** in the Sasso Caveoso is set up as it would have been in the past, with a bed, a corner for pigs and chickens, an area for manure and straw, a trough for the mule and a terracotta chamber pot.

THE NEW TOWN

In contrast to the Sassi is the **Piazza Vittorio Veneto,** the heart of the new town, a smart and spacious square overlooked by cafés, Baroque churches and elegant palazzi. In the evenings this is where you'll see the *passeggiata*. Below the piazza lies the **Palombaro Lungo**, a giant cistern which can be visited on guided tours. Dramatically located on a spur between the two Sassi the Romanesque-style **Cattedrale di Matera**

View of the Sassi from acrooss the gorge

(daily 9am–6pm; free) has a handsome golden-stone facade with a fine rose window. The interior was remodelled in elaborate Baroque style.

PARCO DELLA MURGIA MATERANA

Across the gorge the **Parco della Murgia Materana** is home to abandoned caves and rock-cut churches – many of them created by monks fleeing from persecution. This is the site of some of the very oldest cave-dwellings. Although you can walk or drive there and leave the car at the top of the hill, it is tricky to reach some of the churches and you may want to join a guided tour. From here there are fabulous views of the Sassi across the gorge.

CHRIST STOPPED AT EBOLI

Carlo Levi, the Italian writer, painter and doctor, likened the Matera region to Dante's *Inferno* in his documentary novel: *Christ Stopped at Eboli* (1945). In 1935–36 Levi was exiled for his anti-Fascist activities to the remote village of Aliano (fictional name of Gagliano), 60km (37 miles) inland from Matera, where he wrote the novel. An account of his experience as a political prisoner and a study of the plight of the peasants which he witnessed in southern Italy, the novel was quickly acclaimed a literary masterpiece. In 1979 the book was adapted into a film. The Biblical landscapes around Matera have made perfect backdrops to several other films including Mel Gibson's *The Passion of The Christ* (2004), Pier Paolo Pasolini's *The Gospel According to St Matthew* (1964) and the James Bond film *No Time to Die* (2021).

Carlo Levi's sister, a doctor, had visited malaria-ridden Matera in 1936 and wrote of *'children with the faces of wizened old men, their bodies reduced by starvation almost to skeletons, their heads crawling with lice and covered with scabs'.* They were suffering from trachoma, malaria and dysentery.

Cycling from Otranto to Leuca along the coast

THINGS TO DO

SPORTS

Puglia has increasing appeal for active visitors, offering all-year biking and hiking and plenty of scope for watersports enthusiasts and beach-lovers.

CYCLING

Cycling is popular in Puglia but avoid July and August when the heat is intense, and the traffic (both cars and bikes along cycleways) is at its worst. The best time for a cycling holiday is spring or autumn. The most challenging and one of the most rewarding regions is the mountainous Gargano peninsula. Further south it's easier cycling along the flat coastland and a gently undulating interior. Cycling is popular in and around the Itria Valley, also in the Salentine cities of Lecce, Gallipoli and Otranto. An increasing number of hotels have bikes for guest use, often with no charge. Alternatively you can hire them in most towns and resorts and it's worth asking at tourist offices for cycle maps with recommended routes. For online maps of cycle paths and itineraries go to www.pisteciclabili.com and click on Apulia.

Several companies specialise in cycling holidays, both self-guided and guided, from half a day to a week or more. Self-guided tours typically include accommodation with breakfast, luggage transport, GPS devices programmed with routes, tracks, detailed maps, route notes, 24-hour assistance and medical and luggage insurance; guided tours, some of which are e-bike tours, will include dinners and probably local food tastings en route.

The following offer biking tours throughout Puglia: 4Cycling 'n Trek (www.4cyclingandtrek.com/en), Ciclovagando (www.

ciclovagando.com) and Puglia Cycle tours (www.pugliacycle-tours.com).

Adriatic Cycleway

The Ciclovia Adriatica (Adriatic Cycle Route) is a national tourist cycle route of about 1300km (808 miles) linking Trieste with Santa Maria di Leuca, Puglia's southernmost tip. The Apulian section extends over 500km (311 miles). South of the Gargagno peninsula the route runs for the most part through flat terrain at sea level and takes you mainly on secondary, rural roads with little traffic.

HIKING

Puglia has hiking trails throughout the region, from the forests of the mountainous Gargano Peninsula to the ancient shepherds' paths and along the rugged coast of Salento. The best time to go is spring or autumn. A popular region for a week's walking is the gently undulating Valle d'Itria, through peaceful olives groves and vineyards, and staying overnight at the characteristic hilltop 'white cities'. Macs Adventure (www.macsadventure.com) organise self-guided short breaks or easy to moderate 64km (40 miles) one-week walking tours, starting in Alborobello and ending at Otranto, with transfers, train journey from Ostuni to Lecce and also accommodation (with one night in a *trullo*) all included in the deal.

WATERSPORTS

Diving. The crystalline waters make for excellent snorkelling and diving, with caves, shipwrecks and rich flora and fauna adding to the attraction. Among the best areas are the Tremiti Islands and Salento. Scuba diving centres can be found at many of the main resorts and typically offer programmes for complete beginners to dive-master level. The Tremiti Diving Center (www.

Diving off the Tremiti Islands

tremitidivingcenter.com) on the Tremiti Islands offers a full day snorkelling as well as scuba courses. At Santa Maria di Leuca on the southern tip of Italy you can dive down to the statue of the Lady of the Two Seas, seeing octopuses, nudibranches and sometimes even seahorses as you go. A deeper dive takes you down to the Torre Vado wreck, a Turkish merchant ship on the seabed or for more experienced divers there are 50m (164ft) dives into the open sea, with shoals of barracuda and large groupers.(Salento Diving, www.salentodiving.it).

Other watersports. With its medium to strong winds and large sandy beaches Salento is the best place for kitesurfing and windsurfing. Schools offer courses for all levels of windsurfing but waves and choppy seas at some beaches are not suitable for beginners. The main spots on the Adriatic are Frassanito and San Foca, and on the Ionian coast Gallipoli, Porto Cesareo, Torre Mozza and Torre San Giovanni.

BEACHES AND BOAT TRIPS

Puglia has 800km (500 miles) of coastline, glorious blue seas and some superlative beaches. But it is by no means all pristine white sands and Riviera-like resorts. Much of the coast is dry, rocky terrain and some of it is lined by unsightly development and dirty beaches. The best of the beaches are those on the Gargano Peninsula and in Salento. Try and avoid the second half of July and the whole of August when the sands are packed with Italian holidaymakers. Some beaches charge a fee for access. In Salento there are some exclusive beach clubs with upmarket facilities and prices to match (a couple of sunbeds with a parasol close to the sea in July or August could set you back €75 and parking may well add another €10).

Many resorts offer boat or yacht excursions to explore coastal grottoes striking rock formations or even dolphin-spotting. Alternatively you can rent a jet-ski, dinghy or motorboat and explore independently.

Poolside at Vair Spa

OTHER ACTIVITIES

Horseriding is a great way to discover the local landscape. The A.S.D. Centro Equestre Parco di Mare equestrian sea park at Montalbano di Fasano, 14km (8.5 miles) east of Fasano (www.parcodimare.com) is a long-established equestrian centre with classes for all levels and excursions to the countryside and coast. In Salento the Centro Equitazione Altosalento (www.equitazionealtosalento.it/en) offers courses from show jumping and dressage to pony games for children. Many of the *masserie* (converted farmhouses) offer horseriding.

Golf is not big here but Puglia has a handful of courses, the best of which is the San Domenico Golf at Savelletri di Fasano (www.sandomenicogolf.com), 66km (41 miles) southeast of Bari. This is a challenging 18-hole course with fine views of the Adriatic. San Domenico Golf owns the luxury Masseria San Domenico and offers substantial discounts on green fees to guests.

SPAS

In the land of olives, almonds and vineyards you can indulge in spa treatments with olive oil, almond oil and red wine. If money is no object opt for a dose of pampering at the award-winning Vair Spa at the luxury Borgo Egnazia (www.borgoegnazia.com). This is a soothing, exclusive, candlelit sanctuary, with personalised consultations and treatments to revitalise mind, body and spirit. The team includes barefoot therapists in trailing robes, nutritionists, artists, musicians and dancers.

The main spa town is Santa Cesarea Terme in Salento, 35km (21 miles) south of Lecce. The springs of sulphurous water, which flow from four caves along the coast, have made it an important thermal centre for specialised medical cures and personalized treatments.

SHOPPING

A region renowned for olive oil, pasta and wine, Puglia is packed with little shops and delis selling gastronomic delights. Most towns have a market once a week, selling fresh fruit, vegetables, seafood, meat and typical Puglian specialities. Markets typically open at 8am and are more or less finished by lunchtime so make an early start.

WHAT TO BUY

Pasta. The local pasta is *orecchiette*, 'little ears'. You can see it being made by hand in the backstreets of Bari's old town and you can learn how to make it from scratch at local cooking classes. Shops all over Puglia sell packets of dried *orecchiette*.

Salumi and Cheese. *Salumerie* (delicatessens) offer a tempting range of cured meats and cheeses. In Bari the Antica Salumeria del Gusto, at Piazza Nicola Balenzano 12/A, is a long-established family-run salumeria and something of a Bari institution, offering a grand feast of Puglian cheeses, including ricotta, burrata and stracciatella as well as cured meats, olive oils and wines. It is difficult to resist an impromptu lunch at the counter while in the region. Il Salumaio, located at Via Piccinni 168 is another one of Bari's wonderful delis to explore.

Taralli. *Taralli*, or small rings, similar in texture to a breadstick or pretzel, are sold all over Puglia. In Lecce's Golosità del Salento dal 1942, at Via A.Petronelli 3, you can find a whole variety from fennel, black olive or poppy-seed flavours

Making orecchiette in Bari

Cartapesta artisan at work in Lecce

to sweet *taralli* which can be dunked in wine. This is an enticing shop, with other specialities such as variously-flavoured extra virgin olive oils, almond-stuffed figs, turnip-top pesto and multicoloured *orecchiette*.

Olive Oil. Puglia produces around 40 percent of Italy's olive oil. It's known for its extra virgin olive oil or 'the green gold of Puglia' and is used in beauty products such as body creams, shampoos and sun lotions as well as for culinary use. Fans can follow the Strada dell'Olio di Puglia (Puglia's Olive Oil Road) extending for 140km (87 miles) in the province of Brindisi, with plenty of opportunities to taste and buy. Bottles or tins of Puglia's oil can be found wherever you go and sometimes there are stalls by the roadside. Look for the estate-bottled high-quality oils. The main extra virgin Puglia olive oil DOP producers are Collina di Brindisi, Dauno DOP in the Foggia region and Terra d'Otranto DOP in Salento.

Wine (see page 107) The full-bodied red Primitivo and Negroamaro are the stars of the region, available from enotecas (wine shops/bars) as well as most food shops. Enotecas are obviously better stocked and have the advantage that you can often sample before buying.

Papier-mâché (*Cartapesta*) Dozens of papier-mâché sculptures decorate churches but they look so like wood, marble or stone, it's impossible to tell the difference. Lecce is the main centre with several *cartapesta* workshops in the old town selling finely-handcrafted statues and figurines. *Cartapesta* dates back to the 17th century when it was used as a cheaper alternative to traditional materials. To learn the craft, join a *cartapesta* class at Laboratorio Cartapesta Riso, Via Vittorio Emanuele II 27, Lecce.

PASTA PERFECT

Pasta is in the DNA of the Cavalieri family. Since 1800 they have been growing their own durum wheat in carefully chosen fields in the heart of Puglia. In 1918 Benedetto Cavalieri set up his Mill and Pasta Factory southeast of Lecce (Pastificio Benedetto Cavalieri, www.benedettocavalieri.it) to produce the perfect durum wheat semolina pasta and the factory has been in the family ever since. The artisanal pastas have won many awards for their excellent grain flavour and a noteworthy chewy texture. Since 2007 the firm has been a Learning Centre of the Slow Food University of Gastronomic Sciences of Pollenzo (Piemonte). Students from five continents attend one-week courses on making pasta. Thirty-four different types of pasta are made here, the favourites being the *route pazze* (crazy wheels) and *spaghettoni* (which is thicker than spaghetti). The factory is not open to the public but its pasta can be bought online.

Linen. In the centre of Lecce, Society, at Via degli Ammirati 6 (www.epiphanysociety.com), sells fine and stylish household linen. Despite the name, this is an Italian brand which creates beautiful tablecloths, stunning bed linen, comfy bathrobes and quality napkins and scarves, which come in a wide range of colours for you to choose from.

> **Siesta time**
>
> Note that shops abide by the local custom of siesta, closing their doors from around 1pm–4.30/5.30pm, then staying open until around 7.30/8pm.

Ceramics and Pottery. The ceramics' capital of southern Italy is the town of Grottaglie, 23km (14 miles) east of Taranto. The ceramics quarter has around 50 workshops, where you can watch the potters at work and choose from pots, vases, tiles, lamps, crockery and ornaments. Avoid afternoons, when the workshops are shut, and Sundays, when less than half are open. The tradition goes back to medieval times and some of the ceramicists still use traditional techniques and designs. The Fasanos at Fasano Ceramiche, Via Francesco Crispi 6, have been creating ceramics since the 19th century and the family tradition carries on today with shops in Milan and Rome as well as Grottaglie. If you are worried about weight when travelling, your purchases can be shipped home to you.

Fashion. Bari is the best place in the area for fashion and its Via Sparano is the place to go for big names in designer boutiques. The Puglia Village outlet at Molfetta (https://pugliavillage.it/en/home) 33km (20.5 miles) northwest of Bari, has over 140 boutiques and shops to find selling designer fashions, accessories, cosmetics and sports equipment. Molfetta can be reached from Bari by train and a shuttle bus service links its station with the outlet.

ENTERTAINMENT

Puglia is not renowned for highbrow entertainment although both Bari and Lecce enjoy a programme of ballet, opera and classical music. Ask at the local tourist office for details.

Bari is a university city and although not renowned for nightlife is the liveliest place to be in Puglia north of Salento. There are excellent restaurants serving seafood and local pasta, a few discos and dozens of bars, many offering exotic cocktails and craft beers, and some with live music. Piazza Mercantile in Old Bari is one of the liveliest spots, with wine bars and restaurants lining the square. On the cultural side the hub of the city is the **Teatro Petruzzelli** (Corso Cavour 12; www.fondazionepetruzzelli.com), a resplendent theatre in the centre of town, staging local and international opera, ballet and concerts. Built in the early 20th century it was destroyed by fire in 1991, rebuilt in the same style and reopened in 2009 after years of criminal and civil law suits. It is the fourth largest theatre in Italy. Bari's oldest theatre is the **Teatro Piccinni** (1854) in Corso Vittorio Emanuele, named after Niccolò Piccinni, the 18th-century composer who hailed from Bari. The Teatro Kursaal Santalucia, a fine late Art Nouveau theatre, reopened in 2021 after a decade of closure to host cinema, theatre and cultural exhibitions.

Monument of Niccolo Piccinni

The **Salento** is emerging as the most popular nightlife destination for the young, particularly in summer on the beaches. Hundreds of young people flock to Gallipoli for the cocktail bars, beach parties, clubs, open-air discos and non-stop dancing, starting in the afternoon. Samsara Beach (Lungomare Galileo Galilei, Baia Verde) is the most famous and crowded for nightlife. Other lively spots with beach nightlife (but not on the scale of Gallipoli) are Porto Cesareo, Santa Maria di Leuca and, on the Adriatic coast, Castro, Santa Terme Cesarea and Castro. The Salento has a rich calendar of festivals and events, enlivening the squares and streets of city centres at night.

Lecce is a university city offering an excellent selection of restaurants and watering holes, from rustic little bars to trendy places with craft beers and exotic cocktails. Some of the bars stage live music. The city's theatre, the **Teatro Politeama Greco** (Via XXV Luglio 30; www.politeamagreco.it) hosts shows and concerts as well as plays. Every April Lecce hosts the **Festival del Cinema Europeo** (Festival of European Cinema) featuring the latest European releases.

> **La passeggiata**
>
> One of the greatest forms of entertainment for Italians is the time-honoured *passeggiata* or ritual evening stroll. Families dress up and take to the main streets or piazzas to admire and be admired. Join the throng, preferably with a gelato in hand. In mid-summer the stroll goes on late into the night.

CHILDREN

The Italians adore children and the Pugliesi are no exception. Although there are few attractions specifically designed for youngsters, the island offers sandy, gently shelving beaches, many of them blue flag. However seas can be quite rough and

La Notte della Taranta in Melpignano

parents should take heed of the warning flags. The small rocky coves are fun for children to explore and older ones who are strong swimmers can enjoy jumping off the rocks into the sea. Polignano al Mare is famous for the Red Bull Cliff Diving contest (see page 49) and has lower rocks for children to jump off. A day's excursion to the Tremiti islands (see page 33) is likely to appeal with boat trips to caves and grottoes, and snorkelling in crystalline waters. Older children will enjoy exploring all the castles. For accommodation you can stay in the hobbit-style *trulli* or *agriturismi* (holiday farms) where children can enjoy outdoor pursuits such as cherry-picking or exploring the countryside on horseback, bike or foot.

The main attraction in Puglia aimed specifically at children is **Zoo Safari**, Via dello Zoosafari, close to Fasano (April–Sept daily 9.30am–3pm, Oct Thurs–Tues 10am–2pm, occasional openings in winter, see calendar on website: www.zoosafari.it). This is a large animal theme park with a drive-through, safari-style park (taking your own car) where giraffes block your way or peer through the car windows. Be prepared for long queues in summer. Neighbouring Fasanolandia is a theme park under the same management, with amusement rides and water slides, but it's not nearly as popular as the Zoo Safari. The other big hit with children (though not tiny ones) are the spectacular caves of Grotte di Castellana (see page 53).

CALENDAR OF EVENTS

This is just a handful of the hundreds of events in Puglia throughout the year. Ask at the local tourist office to find out what's on.

January–April Il Carnevale di Putignano, one of Europe's oldest carnivals, with various events up to Shrove Tuesday including four parades, parties and mocking masquerades. Some events also take place in summer. A mini summer carnival also takes place in early July.

March–April Easter week with processions and passion plays throughout Puglia.

First half of April Lecce hosts the European Film Festival (six days).

Late April Bari International Film Festival (one week).

7th–9th May Bari celebrates the three-day La Festa di San Nicola, when thousands of pilgrims from all over the world descend on the city.

8th–10th May La Festa di San Cataldo held in Taranto. Three days of celebration, honouring the city's patron saint.

End of June Danza delle Tarantole (Dance of the Tarantella) at Galatina.

July Fasano Music Festival. Otranto three-day Jazz Festival at the castle; La Ghironda, Ostuni festival.

Mid-July for two months Bari in Jazz Festival in the capital and other towns.

Mid-July to early Aug Festival della Valle d'Itria at Martina Franca: classical music festival, including opera.

August 2–3 weeks La Notte della Taranta in Melpignano is the largest of several events across Salento, celebrating the tarantella dance. Concerts, bands, dancing, folk-music.

Mid-August Festival of the Holy Martyrs in Otranto commemorates the 1480 massacre of 800 residents by Turkish forces.

Late August Festa di Sant'Oronzo in Lecce, dedicated to the town's patron saint. Musical events, food stalls and fireworks. Fish festival in Polignano a Mare.

Late September Commemorations in San Giovanni Rotondo on the anniversary of the passing of Padre Pio (1968). Monte Sant'Angelo festival.

December Christmas festivities, religious events, nativity scenes.

FOOD AND DRINK

Eating out is one of the great pleasures of a holiday in Puglia. What's more, provided you don't tuck into too many *pasticciotti* (egg-custard pies), it's a healthy diet, based on vegetables, fruit, extra virgin olive oil, pasta made with durum flour (high in protein and melatonin) and fish fresh from the sea. The vast plains of Puglia produce abundant fruit, vegetables and wheat, the 60 or so million olive trees yield 40 percent of Italy's olive oil exports and the vines produce 17 percent of Italy's total wine production.

The local cuisine is the deeply-rooted *cucina povera*, the so-called 'poor cuisine', though nowadays it's a fashionable renaissance of cheap and abundant staples. The best known dishes, such as (eggless) pasta with chickpeas, broad bean purée with wild chicory or mussels baked with potato and rice, are based on the humblest ingredients. Seasonality and freshness of ingredients are key.

In a region with 800km (500 miles) of coastline, fish and seafood obviously play a major role in the local cuisine and on most menus fish will predominate over meat.

WHERE TO EAT

Main meals are served in a *ristorante*, *trattoria* or *osteria* but the difference between the three is negligible these days. An *osteria*, traditionally a tavern or inn serving wine and pasta, can nowadays range from traditional to hip. A pizzeria often extends to pasta and meat dishes and the better ones serve pizza bubbling hot from a wood-fired brick oven. The Italians prefer to eat pizza in the evening and to accompany it with beer rather than wine. *Pizza al taglio*, sold by the slice, is a popular takeaway. For a quick bite go to a bar or café where you can find a selection of

Ricci di mare

rolls and sandwiches. Standing at the bar (*al banco*) is always cheaper than sitting at a table with waiter service. An *enoteca* or wine bar will have a serious selection of wines, many available by the glass, and an optional platter of cheese or cold meats to accompany them.

As in the rest of Italy, restaurants offer four courses: *antipasti* (starters), the *primo* (first course, typically pasta but also risotto or soup), the *secondo* (main course of fish or meat) and the *dolce* (dessert), followed perhaps by cheese, an *espresso* and a *digestivo*. Not that you would be expected, these days, to wade through every course. Set menus vary from a basic two or three-course meal, usually with a choice of meat or fish, to a seven-course blow-out *menu degustazione* giving you the chance to try several house specialities. All set menus include service and cover charge; some also throw in house wine, mineral water and coffee. Some of the smaller restaurants don't have menus at all and may bring

Puglia on a plate: sundried tomatoes, salami and taralli

out seemingly never-ending courses without telling you what they are going to be. This is where a few words of Italian could be very useful.

WHAT TO EAT

Antipasti

Antipasti, or starters, are often the highlight of the meal, enabling you to sample several of the local specialities. Most menus offer an impressive array including seafood, *salumi* (cold cuts), cheeses and vegetables. The irresistible *antipasti di mare* is a selection of seafood, typically *gamberoni* (large prawns), *calamari* (squid), *vongole* (clams), *cozze* (mussels) and *polpo* (octopus). A platter of assorted *salumi,* such as wafer-thin slices of *prosciutto crudo* (dry-cured ham), salami, seasoned sausages and *bresaola*, will come with fresh crusty bread and extra virgin olive oil. Vegetable antipasti are likely to feature *peperoni* (peppers), *zucchini* (courgettes), *melanzane* (aubergine or eggplant) and *carciofi* (artichokes). A good way of trying a wide range of local specialities is to choose the *antipasto misto* (mixed starter) which could be a dozen different dishes. This is a meal in itself – or at least one to be shared.

Il primo

Most of Puglia's pasta is made from just flour and water, a tradition which goes back to the time when eggs were beyond the pockets of the Pugliesi. The pasta is nicely chewy and flavoursome and comes in all shapes and sizes. *Orecchiette* or 'little ears' are shaped to hold the sauce and this remains the region's signature pasta, most frequently cooked *con cime di rapa*, translated on menus as 'turnip tops' but more like broccoli. *Orecchiette* and other pastas come with *pomodori e ricotta forte* (tomatoes and double-fermented ricotta), *pomodori, cipolli e capocollo* (cherry tomatoes, red onions and diced *capocollo* [dried cured pork]) or with *ragù di carne* (meat sauce). Seafood pastas are prevalent and often a delicious treat to try in the area of Puglia. They are often made with fresh clams, *calamari*, prawns, lobster or other types of seafood.

Soups can be a meal in themselves, especially the delicious *zuppa di pesce* (fish soup), more of a stew than a soup, or *pancotto*, a broth thickened with bread.

RICCI DI MARE

Well worth trying are *i ricci di mare* (sea urchins), available in spring and autumn. (Don't confuse them with *ricci di terra*, which are hedgehogs.) Locals tend to love them, tourists love or loathe them. Locally they are considered something of a delicacy, because of the time it takes to collect them and the tiny amount of edible fish in each urchin. They are also tricky to open unless you have the right tool. The part you eat is often called the 'roe' but in fact it's the gonads that produce the eggs rather than the eggs themselves. In Bari you can buy them by the port, freshly caught and cracked open by the fishermen, so that you eat them raw – the fresher the better. Don't let the spiny exteriors put you off! They are also used to cook with pasta or risotto but don't be surprised if you only get a tiny quantity of the orange pulp on your pasta.

Il secondo

Along the coasts fish fans are spoilt for choice. The selection of main courses ranges from stuffed or skewered cuttlefish, grilled or steamed octopus to seabass, swordfish and tuna. Fish comes simply grilled, lightly fried or baked, often with a crust. *Fritto misto di mare* is mixed fried fish, normally including *calamari*, anchovies and prawns. In Bari and elsewhere the Spaniards left their mark with *tiella*, a pie layered with rice, potatoes, vegetables, meat or seafood. A basic version of *patate, riso e cozze* (potatoes, rice and mussels) is a filling and very reasonably priced dish. In many restaurants smaller fish are served whole at a set price whereas the larger will be charged by the *etto* (100g). It's quite normal to ask to see the size of a portion first and check the price.

Menus are mainly fish-focussed but most will feature a handful of meat options. Traditional meats are chicken, lamb and kid but don't be surprised to see horse, donkey or slow-cooked offal on menus. Beef was a luxury in the past but with the advent of tourism steaks now often feature on menus. Martina Franca's speciality is *capocollo* (dry-cured pork, see page 57). Just to the east, the hilltop town of Cisternino is known for butchers-cum-tavernas where you queue up to choose your meat and have it roasted or grilled. The speciality is *le bombette*, little pork rolls, filled with yet more pork, breadcrumbs and sometimes spice. There are many different versions.

Vegetables

Puglia produces superb vegetables (*contorni*). A local favourite is the deliciously smooth chicory and broad-bean purée, usually served as a starter and drizzled with extra virgin olive oil. Popular too is *parmigiano di melanzane* made with layers of sliced, fried aubergine, tomato sauce and cheese and baked in the oven. The most commonly found vegetables are *cime di rapa* (turnip greens), *fava* (broad beans), *ceci* (chickpeas, often preserved for the winter months), *cavolo* (cabbage) and *finocchio* (fennel) – as well as the antipasti vegetables (see above). When it comes to mushrooms pride of place goes to the huge Cardoncelli, which grow in the Murgia region near Bari in central Puglia. These are very versatile and are used in rich pasta sauces or stuffed with breadcrumbs, garlic and parsley, layered with potatoes and onions, sprinkled with breadcrumbs and baked in an earthenware dish.

Although it's not always easy to find restaurants that specialise in vegetarian or vegan fare, most can serve vegetable antipasti and a pasta with vegetables.

Cheese

Caciocavallo is a pear-shaped cow's-milk cheese, named 'horse cheese' as it is traditionally hung to mature over a pole known as the *cavallo* ('horse'). The longer it hangs the more flavour it has. *Caciocavallo podolico* is notoriously expensive, aged in caves for months and made exclusively from the milk of Podolica cows that feed on wild herbs and give it its distinctive flavour. More common is *mozzarella*, a traditional southern Italian cheese made from Italian buffalo's milk. *Burrata* is a deliciously creamy fresh cheese, made with buffalo

Orecchiette al ragù di carne

Pecorino from Vieste

or cow's milk – the fresher you eat it the better it tastes. It is often served with pasta. Make sure to look out too for aged, crumbly *pecorino* made from sheep's milk, which sometimes comes with peppercorns as well and is a delight to try.

Desserts

Italians don't excel at desserts (*dolci*) and often skip this course in favour of an ice cream at the local *gelateria*. The choice is often limited to fruit or ice cream, maybe a slice of almond tart, or, in the fancier places, desserts such as tiramisù.

Pastries popular with Pugliesi, especially for breakfast, are *cornetti* (croisssants) with custard cream or other fillings and *pasticciotti*, little pies made with shortcut pastry and filled with ricotta or custard. They are preferably eaten warm and are a great way to start the morning.

COOKERY COURSES

In Bari you can join a half-day walking tour combining sightseeing with a cookery class, learning how to make *orecchiette* from scratch. Lecce has the best choice of cookery courses, ranging from half a day to a week. The Awaiting Table (www.awaitingtable.com) offers week-long courses focusing on cookery and wine, held in Lecce or at a castle an hour south of the city. A shorter cookery course will typically include a visit to the market for local seasonal produce, a hands-on cookery class and a lunch or dinner with fine wines of Salento (see Cooking Experience, www.cookingexperience.it/en). Some of Puglia's wineries are open for tastings and tours. See the Puglia section at Winerist (www.winerist.com) for details and guided tours.

DRINKS

Most Italians prefer to drink mineral water (*acqua frizzante, con gas* or *gassata* all mean sparkling water, *non gassata* or *acqua naturale* is still). *Spremuta* is a freshly-squeezed juice, made with locally-grown oranges or lemons. Italian beer is excellent: ask for a *birra nazionale* and you will probably be served a bottle of Peroni. Many imported brands are also available, especially Kronenbourg and Heineken. Draft beer (*birra alla spina*) is imported and quite pricey. Recent years have seen a growth in the number of craft beers. Numerous bars and particularly cocktail bars serve an *aperitivo* which comes with a complimentary selection of savouries.

Wine

Puglia yields around 15 percent of Italy's wine. With sun-baked vineyards and volcanic red soil it produces large, spicy reds as well as a few whites. Traditionally the emphasis has been on quantity rather than quality with much of the red made by large cooperatives to dispatch to the north to bump up the strength of better-known wines. More recently however this once-backward part of Italy has been producing some serious drinking wines and harnessing native grape varieties to that end.

Puglia's major wine district is Salento, and the three main grape varieties are all reds: Negroamaro, Primitivo and Malvasia Nera. The best Primitivo, which comes from the Manduria region, is rich, fruity and dark-coloured, almost identical to California's Zinfandel

Harvesting Primitivo grapes

(the climates are very similar). Beware of the very high alcohol level. The hot summer sun encourages sugar in the grapes – the minimum strength is 14° but it can often be higher. Look out also for DOC Salice Salentino, produced primarily from the Negroamaro grape and named after the eponymous town. The ripe and robust wine goes very well with red meat and hard cheeses such as pecorino. The best-known white wine is called Locorotondo, named after the lovely hilltop town. In Matera every wine list will feature DOCG Aglianico del Vulture, the main wine of the region of Basilicata. It is a powerful and complex red from the Aglianico grape, which is grown in and around the extinct volcano Mount Vulture.

The cheapest wine in a restaurant is called the *vino della casa* (house wine). It is often served in jugs of *a litro* (litre) or *mezzo litro* (half litre). It is very variable and a great addition to any meal in the region.

TO HELP YOU ORDER

A table for one/two/three **Un tavolo per una persona/per due/per tre**
I would like... **Vorrei...**
The bill, please. **Il conto, per favore.**
Do you have a set menu? **Avete un menù a prezzo fisso?**
I'd like a/an/some... **Vorrei...**

- beer **una birra**
- bread **del pane**
- butter **del burro**
- coffee **un caffè**
- fish **del pesce**
- fruit **della frutta**
- ice cream **un gelato**
- meat **della carne**
- milk **del latte**
- pepper **del pepe**
- potatoes **delle patate**
- salad **un'insalata**
- salt **del sale**
- soup **una minestra**
- sugar **dello zucchero**
- tea **un tè**
- water **dell'acqua**
- wine **del vino**

MENU READER

- **aglio** garlic
- **agnello** lamb
- **albicocche** apricots
- **aragosta** lobster
- **arancia** orange
- **bistecca** beefsteak
- **braciola** chop
- **calamari** squid
- **crostacei** shellfish
- **fegato** liver
- **formaggio** cheese
- **frutti di mare** seafood
- **funghi** mushrooms
- **maiale** pork
- **manzo** beef
- **mela** apple
- **melanzane** aubergine
- **merluzzo** cod
- **ostriche** oysters
- **pollo** chicken
- **pomodori** tomatoes
- **prosciutto** ham
- **tacchino** turkey
- **tonno** tuna
- **uovo** egg
- **uva** grapes
- **verdure** vegetables
- **vongole** clams

# WHERE TO EAT

Price for a two-course meal for one person, including a glass of wine and service charge:

€€€€ over 50 euros
€€€ 35–50 euros
€€ 25–35 euros
€ below 25 euros

THE GARGANO PENINSULA

Monte Sant'Angelo

Medioevo €€ *Via Castello 21; tel: 0844 565356; www.ristorantemedioevo.it*; L and D, closed Mon except Aug–Sept, closed 15–30 Nov. In the historic centre (accessed by foot only) this excellent-value restaurant focuses on local ingredients and regional specialities including home-made pastas such as *troccoli* and aubergine *involtini* or *orecchiette medioevo*, pasta with rocket, pecorino and lamb. Good choice of Pugliese wines.

Peschici

Al Trabucco da Mimì €€€ *Località Punta San Nicola, Peschici; tel: 0884 962556; www.altrabucco.it*; L and D, closed winter. Gorgeous spot on the sea and hugely popular for sunset *aperitivi*. Go for freshly cooked fish and seafood, and a very laid-back atmosphere. Vegetarian options include *fave cicorie*, broad beans and wild chicory. This is one of around a dozen *trabucci* along the coast: wooden contraptions suspended over the sea, traditionally used to net fish.

Rodi Garganico

L'Operetta Osteria di Mare € *Largo Masaniello 10, Rodi Garganico; tel: 338 294 9480;* Mon–Sat 10am–midnight, Sun from 9am. Set on a square in the old town, this *osteria* has a spacious terrace overlooking the beach, harbour and sea. You won't have to agonise over the choice of dishes – it's either the fish or meat menu, both four courses with generous portions at low prices. Staff speak limited English.

Vieste

Il Capriccio €€€ *Località Porto Turistico, Vieste; tel: 0884 705073;* www.ilcapricciodivieste.it*; daily lunch and dinner.* Come for lovely harbour views and some superb fish creations from Chef Leonardo Vescera. Try monkfish in a pistachio and bread crust with orange and cherry sauce or fresh ravioli with sea urchins and *burrata* (creamy mozzarella), followed by one of the sumptuous desserts. There is also a sushi bar and a wine bar.

PUGLIA IMPERIALE

Trani

Quintessenza €€€€ *Via Lionelli 62, tel: 0883 880948;* www.quintessenzaristorante.it*; L and D Mon, Wed–Sat, L only Sun.* Splash out here on some of the best cuisine in southern Italy. Innovative interpretations of classic Puglian dishes – all artfully presented – have earned self-taught Stefano a Michelin star. For a range of specialities opt for one of the tasting menus with wine pairings. Expect the likes of ceviche of grouper with plums and rhubarb, marinated amberjack with tomato and beetroot or tortelli with ricotta, red prawns and Trani Muscat bisque.

BARI AND BEYOND

Bari

L'Osteria del Borgo Antico €€ *Piazza Mercantile, 15, tel: 080 521 0124; mobile: 335 7709 805; L and D Thurs–Tues.* A buzzing and friendly *osteria* on the beautiful Piazza Mercantile, with an outdoor terrace for watching the world go by. Starters include antipasti to share, pastas feature Puglian *cavatelli* and *orrechiette*, or try the regional speciality of *patate, riso e cozze* (potatoes, rice and mussels). Fresh fish includes *gamberini*, cuttlefish on a skewer or delicious grilled seabass. Good pizzas too, which go down well with the house Primitivo.

Panificio Fiore € *Strada Palazzo di Città 38; tel: 080 523 6290;* Mon–Wed and Fri–Sat 8am–2pm and 5–8pm, Thurs and Sun 8am–2pm. Just behind the Basilica di San Nicola this is a bakery rather than a restaurant but it's a great spot for *focaccia*, fresh from the oven, either classic tomato or other flavours. It's one of the oldest and most popular bakeries in Bari – so be prepared to queue. Buy a beer (sold here) and take your snack to one of the benches on the seafront.

Polignano a Mare

Primi e Vini €€ *Piazza Caduti di Via Fani, 7; tel: 080 9680 984;* Thurs–Tues L and D. Not in the old historic centre (where prices tend to be higher) but on a pleasant square with an outdoor terrace, this is a small unpretentious place with a simple setting and friendly waiters who will happily guide you through the menu. Try the warm seafood salad, the *trofie con salsiccia e scamorza* (corkscrew-like pasta with sausage and scamorza cheese) or *orecchiette con ragù di capriolo* (pasta with venison *ragù*).

Savelletri

Ristorante Albachiara €€ *Contrada Lamascopone, Fasano; tel: 339 536 5659.* On the rocky coast between Savelletri and Torre Canne, this is a laidback, fairly basic place with a glorious setting overlooking the turquoise sea. Try tender grilled octopus, mixed seafood or home-made pasta with sea urchins, accompanied by the house rosé. Waiters are friendly and it's a good spot for a family seaside lunch.

VALLE D'ITRIA
Alberobello

L'Aratro €€€ *Via Monte San Michele 25–29, Alberobello, tel: 080 4322789; daily 12.30–3pm and 7.30–11pm; www.ristorantearatro.it/en.* Don't be put off by the touristy street, in the main *trulli* quarter of Alberobello. This is a characterful, rustic restaurant, converted from a complex of *trulli* and with a garden for dining at the back. Specialising in slow food, it offers an excellent range of Puglian specialities displaying names of the local providers. Starters feature local cheeses and *salume* or seafood from the Adriatic. For pasta try *cavatellucci di Terra Madre*, pasta with cherry tomatoes, red onions and diced *capocollo* (dry cured pork), served on a bed of mashed broad beans and wild chicory. Wine labels number to around 100 – mainly from local vineyards.

Ceglie Messapica

Osteria Pugliese € *Vico 1 Orto Nanna Vecchia 10, Ceglia Messapica; tel: 0831 377 115;* Thurs–Tues L and D. It is not surprising that this no-frills, family-run osteria in the historical centre is packed with locals. Prices are exceptionally low for the authentic local fare and the atmosphere is homely and congenial. Don't miss out on the antipasti – which is almost a meal in itself with around a dozen dishes including regional cheeses, charcuterie and vegetables.

Cisternino

Da Zio Pietro € *Via Duca d'Aosta 3, Cisternino;* tel: 080 *444 8300;* daily 6pm– midnight, Sun also 12–3pm. Carnivores will love this butcher-cum-deli-cum-restaurant in the charming hilltop town of Cisternino. You choose your locally sourced meat to be cooked in a wood-burning oven, then tuck in at tables inside or out and wash it down with remarkably cheap house wine. This has been a family butcher business since 1935 and it is very popular. Get there in the early evening or be prepared to queue. No bookings are taken.

Martina Franca

Garibaldi Bistrot €€€ *Piazza Plebiscito 13, Martina Franca; tel: 080 483 7987;* daily L and D. The setting overlooking the Basilica di San Martino, the friendly, helpful service, flavoursome dishes and favourable prices make this one of the most popular restaurants in the centre. Don't miss the house antipasti with creamy *burrata* cheese, cured meats, vegetarian and other local dishes which keep flowing from the kitchen (one between two is plenty!).

Macelleria Braceria Granaldi €–€€ *Via Vincenzo Bellini 108, Martina Franca; tel: 080 698 7892;* Mon–Sat 8–11.45pm (dinner only). Carnivores look no further. Choose your meat to be grilled from the butcher's counter and enjoy it in the simple little restaurant upstairs or outside on the street. The choice includes succulent steaks, tender roast lamb, belly pork slices, slow-cooked offal and *bombette* – little pork rolls filled with more meat, cheese, and breadcrumbs and cooked on a skewer. It all goes down well with a bottle of Primitivo di Manduria.

Nausikaa €€€ *Vico Arco Fumarola 2, Martina Franca; tel: 080 485 8275;* www.ristorantenausikaa.it; Tues–Sun noon–3pm and 8–11pm. This gem of a restaurant, on a side street of the old town, is run by brothers Martino and Francesco whose early training in Puglian cuisine came from their grandmother many years ago. Their bold and imaginative interpretations of traditional Salentine dishes, all beautifully presented, live up to the brothers' maxim: Trasformiamo il cibo in poesia (We transform food into poetry).

Ostuni

Osteria del Tempo Perso €€€€ *Via Gaetano Tanzarella Vitale 47, Ostuni; tel: 0831 304819;* www.osteriadeltempoperso.com. In the historic centre of Ostuni, this long-established *osteria* is divided into two dining areas, one of which is an evocative 500-year-old cave, formerly used as a bakery. Cured meat from Martina Franca, stuffed cuttlefish or *burrata* cheese with pomegranate can be followed by local pastas such as *orecchiette* with clams and courgette flowers or *laganari* with *cardoncelli* mushrooms and chicory. Mains include seabass and steak and there are also vegetarian and gluten-free dishes. Reservations are advisable, particularly for cave-dining.

SALENTO

Brindisi

Cozza Nera €–€€ *Via Schiavone 19, Angolo via Appia; tel: 0831 560 752;* Tues–Sat 11am–3pm and 7–11pm, Sun 11am–3pm. Come for generous helpings of simple fish dishes such as *frittura mista* (mixed fried fish), *riso con patate e cozze* (rice with potatoes and mussels) or *spigola in crosta di mandorle* (seabass in an almond crust), prepared in front of you and served on plastic plates or silver foil trays. Good choice for a quick bite. Fish only.

WHERE TO EAT | 115

Gallipoli

Matre €€€ *Via Antonietta de Pace 116, Gallipoli; tel: 0833 264430;* main restaurant daily 7.30–midnight (dinner only). For fine dining in the centre of Gallipoli look no further. It's well worth splashing out on the seven-course fish tasting menu comprising five antipasti, including the local purple shrimps *(gamberi viola)*, a pasta, perhaps *tortelli* with lobster, plus a dessert.

Lecce

Alle due Corti €€ *Corte dei Giugni 1 (corner of Via Prato), Lecce; tel: 0832 242223;* Mon–Sat 12.30–2.10pm and 7.45–10.30pm; www.alleduecorti.com. Famous for the now fashionable *cucina povera* (food of the poor) this is run by renowned chef, Rosalba De Carlo. Her ancient Salentine dishes are based on the humblest of ingredients: *ciceri and tria* (pasta with chickpeas), *fave nette cu le cicureddhe* (broad bean purée with wild chicory) and *taieddha* (mussels, potatoes and rice, baked in the oven) – all washed down with jugs of Negroamaro house wine.

Trattoria Le Zie € *Via Colonnello Archimede Costadura 19, Lecce; tel: 0832 245178;* closed all day Mon and Sun D. The small, quaint dining room, full of pictures and photos and dating back to 1966, feels like a family home and is popular with locals. The aunts *(Le Zie)* produce authentic, home-made food with simple dishes such as meatballs (a real favourite), fava bean purée with chicory, stuffed squid or stewed octopus. It is very popular so make sure to book in advance – if you don't speak any Italian ask a local to do it for you.

Otranto

L'Altro Baffo €€€ *Via Cenobio Basiliano 23; Otranto; tel: 083 6801636;* www.laltrobaffo.com; daily 12.30–3pm and 7.30–11pm. Tuck into raw or cooked fish antipasti, carbonara of sea urchins or a platter of prawns, langoustines and local lobster at this small, family-run restaurant. Young chef Cristina Conte, along with her mother and sister, produce creative new versions of traditional Salentine seafood recipes. The setting is simple and stylish, with a small terrace for alfresco dining.

L'Approdo di Enea € *Via Porto, Porto Badisco; tel: 347 5823163;* L and D daily. Simple but tasty little trattoria at the lovely secluded bay of Porto Badisco south of Otranto, where, according to Virgil, Aneas (Enea) first landed on Italian shores. Make sure to tuck into *linguini ai ricci* (with sea urchins) or *spaghetti alle vongole* (with clams) and enjoy gorgeous sea views while you dine.

BASILICATA

Matera

Alle Fornace €€ *Piazza Cesare Firrao tel: 0835 335 037*. This sober-looking spot in the new town is one of the few places in Matera to specialize in seafood. Dishes are traditionally prepared but come with creative twists, such as *baccal con polenta* (cod with polenta). A great little restaurant for a delicious meal.

L'Abbondanza Lucana €€€ *Via Bruno Buozzi 11, Matera; tel: 0835 334574;* closed Mon and D on Sun. Take a tour of Basilicata cuisine with the antipasti misti and you will realise why this restaurant is called 'L'Abbondanza Lucana' (Abundance from Basilicata). The antipasti, home-made pasta and mains, which include slow-cooked pork cheeks and tender wild boar, go well with the local, full-bodied Aglianico del Vulture wine, dubbed 'the Barolo of the south'. The setting is an elegant series of caves, with a terrace for outdoor eating.

Baccus €€ *Vico Santa Cesarea 34 (Angolo Via D'Addozio), Matera; tel: 0835 1880536;* Tues–Sun L and D; www.ristorantebaccus.it. On the edge of Matera's Sassi (ancient cave-dwellings) Baccus has a romantic partial-cave setting as well as outdoor tables at a rustic terrace. The superb house antipasti is enough for a whole meal for two, which consists of cheeses, cured meats, *peperoni cruschi* (crushed peppers) and ricotta soufflé. For a pasta try *taglioni* with *cicerchie* (seeds of the chickling vetch), *cardoncelli* mushrooms and peppers or *foglie d'ulivo*, a local leaf-shaped pasta with tomatoes, arugula, pancetta and ricotta. It all goes down well with the house Primitivo wine of course, so make sure to order a glass while you tuck into your food.

TRAVEL ESSENTIALS

PRACTICAL INFORMATION

A Accommodation	118
Airports	119
B Bicycle rental	119
Budgeting	120
C Camping	121
Car hire	121
Climate	122
Clothing	122
Crime and safety	122
D Driving	123
E Electricity	124
Embassies and consulates	124
Emergencies	124
G Getting there	124
Guides and tours	125
H Health and medical care	125
L Language	126
LGBTQ travellers	126
M Maps	127
Media	127
Money	127
O Opening hours	128
P Police	128
Post offices	129
Public holidays	129
R Religion	129
T Telephone	130
Time zones	130
Tipping	131
Toilets	131
Tourist information	131
Transport	132
Travellers with disabilities	133
V Visa and entry requirements	133
W Websites and internet access	134
Y Youth hostels	134

A

ACCOMMODATION

Puglia has plentiful accommodation ranging from stylish boutique hotels and villas to simple B&Bs and farms. For peaceful getaways there is the option of *masserie*, traditional farmhouses which have been restored and converted into tourist accommodation. In the last 20 years or so these have been very much part of the rapid rise in tourism in Puglia. They range from basic *agriturismo*-style family farms to sophisticated five-star hotels, often in rustic style, with suites in villas and outbuildings, a peaceful pool and perhaps a private beach, golf course and/or spa treatments. Most lie within 15 minutes' drive or so from nearby towns or attractions but they are typically in seemingly remote locations amid olive groves and vineyards. A hired car is advisable – especially if you don't intend to dine in every evening. Most of the *masserie* serve meals, often sumptuous ones featuring Puglian specialities with food sourced straight from the farm or from small local suppliers. Many of Puglia's iconic *trulli* (see page 52) in the Valle d'Itria have also been converted to guest accommodation, with modern-day facilities. These squat conical houses range from *de luxe* conversions to something more akin to the original peasant-farmer dwelling. B&Bs and Airbnbs are plentiful in Puglia. Simple self-catering facilities are often provided which can save on restaurant costs and enable those with specific dietary requirements to choose and cook their own ingredients.

During the high season accommodation in popular resorts along the coast should be booked ahead, especially in July and August. Prices drop dramatically off-season (between 30 and 50 percent) but bear in mind that many resorts close in winter. Savings can also be made by staying a few kilometres away from the coast or out of town. For details of *agriturismi*, *masserie* and other rural accommodation go to the Puglia section of Agriturismo.net (www.agriturismo.net). Charming Puglia (www.charmingpuglia.com/en) have a decent selection of excellent hotels, *trulli* and *masserie* to browse through.

AIRPORTS

Bari's Karol Wojtyla Airport, named after the late Pope John Paul II and also known as Palese Airport (www.aeroportidipuglia.it), is 10km (6 miles) northwest of Bari city centre. Terravision in conjunction with Autoservizi Tempesta provide a shuttle bus service to Central Station in Bari (€4 one way) which takes about 30 minutes and operates from 05.35am to 12.10am. Tickets can be bought on board the bus. AMTAB Line 16 is the cheapest bus service (€1 one way) but far slower, with frequent stops. Tickets can be purchased from the newsagent inside the terminal building. Bari airport is on the metropolitan rail service (the F2 line) which takes just 20 minutes to get to Bari central station but it is a good 10-minute walk to the station from the airport through a series of tunnels. Trains run from 05.26am to 11.38pm every 20 or 30 minutes. Tickets (€5 one-way) can be bought online at www.ferrovienordbarese.it or at the station. Pugliairbus (www.aeroportidipuglia.it; click on Bari then transport) connects the airports of Bari, Brindisi, Foggia and Taranto, also to Matera in Basilicata. A taxi to the centre of Bari from the airport takes 20–25 minutes and costs around €25.

Brindisi's **Salento Airport** (www.aeroportidipuglia.it) is a small airport 4km (2.5 miles) from the city centre. Ryanair is currently the only airline flying directly from the UK (out of Stansted and Manchester). A bus runs into the city centre every 30 minutes, taking around half an hour (€4). There is also a direct and cheap bus service to Lecce. A taxi (€20) takes around 15 minutes to the centre.

B

BICYCLE RENTAL

(See also Cycling in What to Do Section) Cycle-hire is widely available and an increasing number of hotels have bikes for guests' use. Scooters and electric bikes as well as trekking, road and hybrid bikes can be hired in most towns and resorts. Tourist information offices can supply names and prices of bike-hire places. Rental costs are typically €15–20 for a day, €35–€45 for three days. Electric bikes are available at an extra cost. Bikes can be taken on regional train services displaying the bike logo but you need to buy a bike ticket. Puglia in Movimento (www.pugliainmovimento.com) is a Bari bike service with free delivery to the airport, railway station or your hotel. Assistance on self-guided bike tours, tour guides, moving luggage day by day and other services are offered.

BUDGETING

Flight prices to Puglia vary hugely, depending on the season, the day of the week and how far in advance you book. A return flight from the UK to Bari with a low-cost carrier costs around €100 in winter, €200–300 in high season (basic flight prices). For a real bargain look for last minute offers, sometimes at ridiculously low prices.

A double room in a budget hotel will cost €60–120 per night, in a mid-range hotel €100–250 and for a luxury *masseria* in high season you can pay as much as €400–700. B&Bs, Airbnb and Agriturismi offer much cheaper accommodation and youth hostels charge €15–25 in a dorm or from €30 for a basic double room. Restaurants in popular resorts, especially with a sea view, might set you back €45 for a three-course dinner with wine, rising to over €100 for one of the top restaurants. Simple trattorias charge much less. Fuel costs are similar to those across Europe but public transport remains inexpensive.

Coffee served at a table costs €1.50–3, a coke or soft drink €2.50–3, a beer €2.50–4, a glass of wine from €3-5, cocktails €6–10. If all you need is to quench your thirst remember that drinks at the bar are cheaper than those served on the terrace.

Museum entrance fees vary from €3–20. Visitors under 18 are entitled to free admission to state museums, those aged 18–25 from the EU are entitled to reduced price tickets. Combined tickets to several sights are available in the major cities. The main centres, such as Bari and Lecce, offer free guided tours of the city.

C

CAMPING

Camping is only permitted in designated sites. Many of the campsites are vast recreational centres with restaurants, pools, bars and sports facilities, often close to the sea. The majority are only open for the summer season, either from

April to October or June to September. Local tourist offices can provide details of sites in the region. For those who don't have their own tent or caravan there are bungalows and static caravans to rent. For details of sites consult Camping.it (www.camping.it/en) or Campeggi.com (https://www.campeggi.com/en).

CAR HIRE

Hiring a car is by far the easiest way to explore Puglia though driving in the towns and cities is not for the faint-hearted. Most major companies such as Avis, Hertz and Europcar have outlets at the airports but it is usually cheaper to book in advance. Car rental costs from around £150 per week for a small car. 'Inclusive' prices do not generally include personal accident insurance or insurance against damage to windscreens, tyres and wheels. Optional excess insurance costs from around €15 a day – it is far cheaper to take out your own excess insurance policy in advance. The minimum age for hiring a car is 21–25, depending on the company, and anyone hiring must have held a valid licence for at least one year. Rental companies will accept your country's national driving licence but you must show your passport or ID. Credit card imprints are taken as a deposit and are usually the only form of payment acceptable. Beware of companies trying to overcharge for petrol when you take the car back, claiming the tank is not full on return. Keep your last petrol receipt just in case you need to challenge them.

Car-hire companies:
Avis: www.avis.com
Budget: www.budget.com
Europcar: www.europcar.com
Hertz: www.hertz.com
Sixt: www.sixt.com

CLIMATE

The heat in July and August can be relentless and it's not unusual for day time temperatures to soar to 40°C (95°F). If you go at this time of year make sure you are close either to a beach or a swimming pool and do as the Italians do and take a siesta in the afternoon. The best times from the point of view of climate and fewer tourists are spring (April–early June), with the added bonus of a profusion of blossom and wildflowers, and early autumn (September–October) after the crowds have gone but while the air and sea are still warm. But beware that the season is short and by late September many coastal hotels and resorts have closed down for winter. The wettest months are from November to February, but rainfall is rarely significant.

CLOTHING

Bring light clothing and a hat during the hot summer months. In spring and autumn you will need a jacket or sweater for the evenings. Winters can be chilly particularly in Gargano's mountainous areas, so bring warm clothes and waterproofs. Shorts are acceptable but bathing attire off the beach is often frowned upon, and wearing miniskirts, skimpy shorts or shoulderless garments in churches may cause offence.

CRIME AND SAFETY

Take precautions against pickpockets, especially in ports such as Bari and Brindisi and take extra care in Taranto. Leave passports, jewellery, large amounts of cash, credit cards you are not using and other valuables in the hotel room safe – if it has one. Keep a copy of your passport and other valuable documents separately in case you need to replace them. Be particularly vigilant at markets, street festivals and on public transport. To protect yourself against Vespa-riding bandits who snatch bags while whizzing by at high speed, carry your bag so it faces away from the street. Never leave valuables in view within your car. If you are robbed report it as soon as possible to the local police. You will need a copy of the declaration in order to claim on your insurance.

D

DRIVING

You do not need an International Driving Permit to drive in the EU if you have a photocard driving licence issued in the UK. The network of roads across the region has much improved though you can still expect potholes on some roads. The main frustrations are negotiating town centres (poor signing to the centre, complex one-way systems and congested streets), finding parking places, following diversion signs (often to avoid town centres) which disappear and keeping your cool with fellow motorists who drive fast and sometimes recklessly.

Rules and Regulations. The speed limit on motorways is 130km/h (80mph), on secondary roads 90km/h (55mph), in towns 50km/h (30mph). Drive on the right, overtake on the left. At intersections and roundabouts traffic on the right has priority. Speeding and other traffic offences are subject to heavy on-the-spot fines. The use of hand-held mobiles while driving is prohibited. The blood alcohol limit is 0.05 percent (the UK limit is 0.08 percent) and police occasionally make random breath tests.

Breakdowns and Assistance. In case of an accident or breakdown, dial 113 (general emergency) or the Automobile Club of Italy on 116. Roadside phones are placed at frequent intervals along major roads.

Parking. Historic centres are often inaccessible to cars, other than those of residents. Look out for ZTL (*zona a traffico limitato*) signs at the entrance to restricted traffic areas, enforced with cameras. You can enter only if you are staying at accommodation within the restricted zone and it is often the case that you can only drop off your luggage, before finding a parking place outside the centre. Enquire in advance from your hotel or B&B. If driving into a historic centre during high season (and in some towns out of it too) the hotel will need to take your registration number and inform the police. Many cities and towns have municipal parking lots and garages, denoted by a white 'P' on a blue background, at the fringes of their historic centres.

Petrol. Petrol and diesel are readily available. Diesel is called *diesel* or *gasolio*, petrol *benzina senza piombo* (also *benzina verde*). Many stations have self-service pumps, available 24 hours.

E

ELECTRICITY

220V/50Hz is standard. Visitors from other countries may require an adaptor and those from North America will need a transformer as well. Sockets are either two- or three round-pins.

EMBASSIES AND CONSULATES

Australian Embassy: Via Antonio Bosio 5, Rome; tel: 06 852 721; http://italy.embassy.gov.au

Canadian Consulate: Via Zara 30, Rome; tel: 06 854441; www.canada.it

Irish Embassy: Villa Spada, Via Giacomo Medici 1, Rome; tel: 06 585 2381; www.dfa.ie/irish-embassy/italy

Honorary Consulate of South Africa, Via Beata Elia di San Clemente, 255, 72122 Bari; tel: 080 524 0388; email: consolato.sudafrica.bari@gmail.com

UK Embassy: Via XX Settembre 80a, Rome; tel: 06 4220 0001; www.gov.uk/world/organisations/british-embassy-rome

US Embassy: Via Vittorio Veneto 121, Rome; tel: 06 46741; https://it.usembassy.gov

EMERGENCIES

The general emergency number is **113**. Call **112** for police, **115** for fire and **118** for an ambulance. For road assistance call **116**.

G

GETTING THERE

Before travelling visitors from the UK should check the entry requirements for Italy at https://www.gov.uk/foreign-travel-advice/italy
Air travel. Puglia is served by low-cost charter and scheduled airlines from the UK and other parts of Europe. British Airways operates flights from Heathrow to Bari and Brindisi; Ryanair flies from London Stansted to Bari daily, and to Brindisi three times a week in season, twice a week in winter; Easyjet runs flights from Gatwick to both airports.

GUIDES AND TOURS

Day-trip itineraries with multilingual guides are available through hotels, tourist offices, local travel agencies and tour operators. In Bari there are guided walking, biking and rickshaw tours, often combining culture with street food. The city has a lively mp3 audio guide combined with a map. Popular destinations for guided day-trips are Lecce for Baroque splendour, Alberobello for quaint *trulli*, Castellana Grotte for spectacular caves and Matera in Basilicata for cave dwellings. Gastronomy is the theme of many tours throughout Puglia, perhaps making (and eating) your own Puglian pasta, visiting an oil press or vineyards with tastings along the way. The official Puglia tourist website (www.viaggiare-inpuglia.it) has details of guided tours and websites of operators.

H

HEALTH AND MEDICAL CARE

Check information on current Covid-19 requirements for Italy on www.gov.uk/foreign-travel-advice/italy/health. Covid-19 updates are also available on the Italian Tourist Board website at http://www.italia.it/en/useful-info/covid-19-updates-information-for-tourists.html. The website also has details of regulations for travelling within Italy and for access to recreational activities and services. Visitors should carry with them the EHIC (European Health Insurance Card) or the GHIC (UK Global Health Insurance Card). The GHIC card is available for free in the UK from the NHS website (www.nhs.uk/using-the-nhs/healthcare-abroad) which entitles you to free medical treatment within the EU. Existing EHIC cards remain valid until the expiry date, after which you need to apply for a GHIC card. The cards cover only medical care, not emergency repatriation costs or additional expenses. It is therefore important to have travel insurance to cover all eventualities. You will be asked to pay for treatment up front, so keep all receipts for reimbursement. In many areas in summer there is a Guardia Medica Turistica (tourist emergency medical service) which functions 24 hours a day. Details are available from pharmacies, tourist offices, hotels and local newspapers.

Pharmacies (*farmacie*) have a green cross sign above the entrance. In each town, one stays open late and on Sundays on a rotating basis. The after-hour locations for the month are posted on the doors of all pharmacies. For serious cases or emergencies, dial 118 for an ambulance or head for the *Pronto Soccorso* (Accident and Emergency) of the local hospital.

Tap water is safe to drink, though, like most Italians, the Pugliesi prefer bottled water.

L

LANGUAGE

English is spoken in hotels and restaurants of main towns and resorts, but once you venture off the tourist track, prepare to communicate in Italian. Standard Italian is spoken throughout the region, but, as elsewhere in Italy, Puglia has its own dialects. One of the most notable is *griko*, a dialect of Greek which is very occasionally spoken by the older generation in the 'Greek villages' of Grecia Salentina, south of Lecce.

LGBTQ TRAVELLERS

Attitudes are more relaxed nowadays and there are LGBTQ hangouts in the main cities, especially Bari where it's easy to find LGBTQ clubs, saunas and cruising spots. Gallipoli is another popular LGBTQ centre, which hosts Salento Pride in mid-August. There are a handful of LGBTQ beaches in Puglia, mainly in the Salento region and including Gallipoli. The national LGBTQ rights organisation is Arci-gay, www.arcigay.it. Gay Friendly Italy (www.gayfriendlyitaly.com) is an English-language website for LGBTQ travellers in Italy, and includes venues in Puglia.

M

MAPS

A good map is essential if you are touring the region since road signs leave much to be desired. The free Touring Editore Puglia Map 1:500.000, provided by many tourist offices, is useful for an overall view but for touring you need a far more detailed map such as the Touring Club Italiano 1:200.000, available from newsstands and bookstores. Tourist offices supply free maps of towns and resorts but for the larger destinations, eg Lecce, it's worth buying a more detailed map which marks all the streets.

MEDIA

Away from the main cities English-language newspapers can be hard to find, especially out of season. The most commonly found are the *Herald Tribune* and *New York Times* International Edition. The centre-left *La Republica* and the right-wing *Corriere della Sera*, both Italian newspapers, publish southern editions. Most hotels now provide English-language television news channels.

MONEY

Currency. The currency in Italy is the euro (€). A euro is divided into 100 cents with 2, 5, 10, 20 and 50 cent coins, and 1 and 2 euro coins. The euro notes are 5, 10, 20, 50, 100, 200 and 500.

Currency Exchanges. Money can be changed at exchange offices and some banks and post offices. Exchange offices *(cambios)* are found in most towns and have the longest opening hours, but banks and post offices normally offer the best rates of exchange.

Credit Cards. Visa and Master Card are the most widely-accepted credit cards and many establishments do not take American Express. Except in smaller villages, major credit cards are accepted by shops, hotels, restaurants and petrol stations. Museums will usually insist on cash. Cards can also be used to pay motorway tolls, but it is advisable also to keep some cash on hand, as the card-reading machines are sometimes out of order.

O

OPENING HOURS

Opening hours of museums, galleries, churches and castles vary widely. Few are open daily. Monday is the most common closing day but for some it's Sunday or occasionally another day of the week. Smaller museums may open for half a day only. Churches are usually closed from noon to 4 or 5pm but don't be surprised to find monuments closed for ongoing restoration or major sites closed without warning. Local tourist boards can provide current opening times for sights in their town or region.

Banks. Mon–Fri 8.30am–1pm or 1.30pm and most are also open 2.30/3pm–4/4.30pm.

Shops. Mon–Sat 8 or 9am–1pm and 4–7.30/8pm, but many non-food shops close on Monday and, with the exception of supermarkets, food shops may close on Wednesday. In main towns and resorts some shops stay open at lunchtime and on Sundays.

Museums. Opening hours vary and constantly change. Most museums are open six days a week, the most common closing day being Monday. Some museums open mornings only on Sundays and holidays. Currently access to most museums is only possible through online ticket purchase and everyone over 12 is required to show a GreenPass, which shows proof of vaccination against Covid-19, recovery from the virus within the last 6 months or a negative test taken within the last 48 hours. Vaccination certificates (in digital or paper form) which are issued in the UK and certain other countries are accepted in lieu of the GreenPass.

P

POLICE
There are three kinds of police in Italy: the *vigili urbani*, who deal with petty crime, traffic, parking and other day-to-day matters; the *carabinieri* who are the armed military police who handle law and order and the *polizia stradale* who patrol the roadways. Any of these forces may answer a 113 emergency call, though the *carabinieri* have their own emergency number, 112.

POST OFFICES
Post offices are generally open Mon–Sat 8.30am–1.30pm and in major cities the main post office is usually open Mon–Sat 8am–6.30pm or later. If you want something to arrive urgently, consider using the more expensive *Postapriority Internazionale*. Stamps are available from post offices but also from tobacconists *(tabacchi)*.

PUBLIC HOLIDAYS
Banks and most shops are closed on the following holidays:
1 January: **New Year's Day** *(Capodanno)*
6 January: **Epiphany** *(Epifania)*

March/April: **Easter Sunday and Monday** (Pasqua e Pasquetta)
25 April: **Liberation Day** (Festa della Liberazione)
1 May: **Labour Day** (Festa del Lavoro)
2 June: **Republic Day** (Festa della Repubblica)
15 August: **Assumption Day** (Ferragosto)
1 November: **All Saints' Day** (Ognissanti)
8 December: **Immaculate Conception** (Immacolata Concezione)
25 December: **Christmas Day** (Natale)
26 December: **Boxing Day** (Festa di Santo Stefano)

R

RELIGION

Like the rest of Italy, Puglia is predominantly Roman Catholic, though only a small percentage of the population regularly attend Sunday Mass. The hours of Mass vary, but each church has its own timetable pinned on its main door. Religious festivals are still very much part of Puglian life and every town has a saint's day, which is celebrated with music, food and wine. Modest dress is expected when visiting places of worship.

T

TELEPHONE

To call an Italian telephone number from outside Italy, either from a landline or mobile, you need to add the international dialling code for Italy which is 0039 (+39), followed by the telephone number you require, including the first 0. For calls within Italy, telephone numbers must be preceded by the area code even if the call is made within the same district. When phoning abroad from Italy dial 00 (the international access code), then the country code, followed by the city or area code omitting the initial 0, and then the desired number. Hotels levy large surcharges on long-distance calls.

Mobile (Cell) Phones. Since the UK left the EU the guarantee of free roaming for UK mobile users has ended. It is now phone operators who decide whether to charge international roaming rates and if so, how much. Check with your company prior to departure. By law customers must be informed when they have used up 80% and 100% of their data allowance. There is also a rule whereby they cannot be charged more than £45 of mobile data charges, unless they have actively opted to continue using data when abroad. If you are being charged and you are making a large number of calls or staying for some time it may be worth purchasing a SIM 'pay as you go' card *(una scheda ricaricabile)* available at shops of the main providers or at post offices.

TIME ZONES

Italy is one hour ahead of Greenwich Mean Time (GMT). From the last Sunday in March to the last Sunday in October, clocks are put forward by one hour. The chart below shows times across the globe when it is midday in Bari.

New York	**Puglia**	Jo'burg	Sydney	Auckland
7am	**noon**	1pm	9pm	11pm

TIPPING

In Italy a service charge of 10–15 percent is usually built into the bill, though a little extra for good service is always appreciated. At a bar, it is customary to leave a coin or two on the counter for a barman. Tip porters one euro per bag. To tip a taxi driver simply round up the total.

TOILETS

Public toilets are hard to find, but you can usually use toilets in cafés and bars. In some cases the toilets are locked and you will have to ask for the key (*la chiave*). Buying a drink at the same time will be appreciated. Major sites now have reasonable facilities. The men's toilets are signed *Uomini* or *Signori*, the ladies' *Donne* or *Signore*.

TOURIST INFORMATION

The website for the Italian National Tourist Board (ENIT) is www.enit.it. The official tourism website for Puglia is www.viaggiareinpuglia.it.

The main tourist offices in Puglia will have staff who speak English but this is often not the case with the smaller information offices. Normal opening hours are daily, all day during the summer, but off-season hours are much shorter. A travel agency or local tour operator can be a good source of advice if the tourist office is closed or non-existent. The following are the tourist offices in the main towns:

Puglia
Alberobello: Via Monte Nero 1, tel: 0804 322 822
Bari: Piazza Ferrarese 29, tel: 0805 242244
Brindisi: Via Duomo 20, tel: 0831 523072
Gallipoli: Via Kennedy, 20, tel: 0833 264283
Lecce: c/o Sedile Comunale, Piazza Sant'Oronzo, tel: 0832 242099
Martina Franca: Piazza XX Settembre, 3, tel: 0804 805702
Ostuni: Corso Mazzini, 8, tel: 0831 339627
Otranto: c/o Castello Aragonese, Piazza Castello, tel: 0836 801436
Taranto: Castello Aragonese, tel: 334 2844 098
Trani: Piazza Trieste, 10, tel: 0883 588 830
Vieste: Piazza Kennedy, 13, tel: 0884 708806
Basilicata
Matera: Piazza Vittorio Veneto, tel: 0835 680254

TRANSPORT

Coach and Bus. Bus services, operated by around 20 different companies, link Puglia's main towns and offer relatively speedy access across the region. Generally speaking coaches are more reliable and quicker than trains and for small towns are often the only option. For details of the different companies and their destinations consult the official tourist website, www.viaggiareinpuglia.it, under the Useful Info section. Note that there are far fewer services on Sundays and holidays.

Ferry. A total of five ferry companies service the Tremiti Islands, off the coast of the Gargano peninsula, which includes Traghetti Lines (www.traghettilines.it), Tirrenia (www.tirrenia.it) and NavLib (www.navlib.it). Boats depart to the islands from various points found on the coast, including Vieste and Peschici in summer. The only year-round service to be found is from Termoli in Molise.

Helicopter. You can fly to the Tremiti Islands from Foggia by helicopter with Alidaunia (www.alidaunia.it).

Rail. Trains are operated by Trenitalia (www.trenitalia.com). The system is cheap but there are fewer high-speed trains and tracks than in the north and the system is often slower and less convenient than bus or coach for seeing the region. Main stations have self-service ticket machines with instructions in English and this is usually quicker than using the ticket office. Travel on InterCity and the high-speed Frecciarossa, Frecciargento, and Frecciabianca trains requires a supplement. Tickets for all trains must be stamped in the yellow machines on the platforms before boarding the train. Failure to do so can incur a hefty on-the-spot fine. Puglia has four regional private lines: Ferrovie del Sud Est (www.fseonline.it) connecting Bari and its south-east province to Brindisi, Lecce and Taranto; Ferrovie Appulo Lucane (www.ferrovieappulolucane.it) running across the province of Bari and the Murgia towns to Basilicata; Ferrotramviaria (www.ferrovienordbarese.it) connecting Bari to its main northern province towns and the Barletta-Andria-Trani province and finally Ferrovie del Gargano (www.ferroviedelgargano.com serving the whole province of Foggia. Tourist offices can provide a free and useful leaflet with a map of the different services. Note that outside high season the train services to popular resorts tend to be less frequent.

Taxi. In cities taxis can be found in main squares, or can be telephoned. The meter should be turned on at the start of the journey. Make sure to be aware of touts without meters who may approach you at airports and large train stations.

Bari: Radio Taxi; 080 554 3333

Lecce: Radio Taxi; 331 241 0613

Uber taxis are also available in Puglia.

TRAVELLERS WITH DISABILITIES

Puglia can present problems for travellers with disabilities. The hilltop towns have steep cobbled streets, many churches and sites have steps and some museums do not have wheelchair access. Given the challenges it is wisest to book through a specialised tour operator or travel agency who can offer customized tours and itineraries, eg Disabled Holidays (www.disabledholidays.com).

V

VISA AND ENTRY REQUIREMENTS

For current entry requirements to Italy, including rules regarding Covid-19, UK citizens should consult www.gov.uk/foreign-travel-advice/italy/entry-requirements. A British passport is sufficient for stays in Italy for up to 90 days. Citizens of the US, Canada, Australia, New Zealand and South Africa also need only a valid passport for stays of no more than 90 days. Visitors should ensure their passport is valid for at least six months beyond the departure date.

W

WEBSITES AND INTERNET ACCESS

Useful sites are:
www.italia.it Italian Government Tourist Board, which covers the whole of country.
www.viaggareinpuglia.it Official tourist website for Puglia.
www.trenitalia.com Trenitalia: Italian State Railways.
www.thelocal.it *The Local*, Italy's news in English.
www.parks.it Italian parks and reserves .
www.thethinkingtraveller.com Specialists on Puglia, offering tailor-made villa rentals and a useful guide to the region.

There are an increasing number of wi-fi hotspots in public places and plenty of cafés with free access are also available. Nearly all hotels and other types of accommodation offer free wi-fi within their premises, though you may find it doesn't extend to all of the guest rooms.

Y

YOUTH HOSTELS

For information and free reservations contact Hostel World (www.hostelworld.com). Nowadays many hostels offer accommodation on a par with that of a budget hotel. Prices are €15–25 for a dorm bed and €30–60 for a simple double room with shared bathroom. See below for recommended hostels in the region and the city centre); Bari; www.olivetreehostel.it.

Host Bari Centrale, Corso Cavour 21 (2.4km from city centre); Bari; tel: 392 9315 745; www.hostelworld.com

Ostello Salento, Via Pirelli 6, Alezio (near Gallipoli); tel: 0833 282 718; www.ostellosalento.com/en.

WHERE TO STAY

Puglia now offers accommodation to suit all tastes: five-star laps of luxury, chic boutique hotels, *masserie* (converted farmhouses), *trulli* hotels, simple guest houses, hostels, apartments and Airbnbs. For popular coastal resorts it is wise to book ahead from Easter through to September, and in July and August it is essential. Off season, rates are often reduced dramatically. Some hotels insist on two or sometimes three-night stays in high season, and occasionally half board. Many of the hotels recommended, particularly the *masserie*, are quite rural and you will need a car.

Tourist Tax (Tassa di Soggiorno) rates and regulations vary from place to place but generally the tax must be paid directly by tourists during their stay. The costs are €1–6 per person per night, up to a maximum of five (or sometimes three) consecutive overnight stays. The rate varies according to the type of accommodation, whether it is a hotel (the more stars the higher the tax), a B&B, campsite or self-catering. Children under 12–14 (the age varies) are exempt from the charge or pay a discounted rate. The charge may only apply for six months of the year, sometimes with a higher rate from July to August.

For more information see under Accommodation in Travel Tips, page 118.

The symbols below are a rough indication of rates per night for a double room with bathroom in high season, including breakfast but excluding tourist tax.

€€€€ over 350 euros
€€€ 200–350 euros
€€ 120–200 euros
€ less than 120 euros

GARGANO

Peschici

La Chiusa delle More €€€ *Località Padula, 1.5km (1 mile) west of Peschici; tel: 330 543 766; www.lachiusadellemore.it; open late May–end Sept.* On a hillside in an ancient olive grove about 1km (half a mile) from the sea, this is a peaceful country hotel, converted from an ancient farmhouse, with exceptionally good food and delightful hosts. Cookery courses are offered in May, June and September.

Vieste

Hotel Seggio €–€€ *Via Vesta,7, Vieste; tel: 0884 708123; www.hotelseggio.it.* In the heart of the old town on the cliffs, this is a friendly, family-run three-star hotel with 22 rooms and fine sea views. It has its own small pool and tiny beach area, accessed by lift. There is no parking but staff will help you find a space and take your bags.

BARI AND BEYOND

Polignano a Mare

Covo dei Saraceni €€€ *Via Conversano 1–1/A, Polignano a Mare; tel: 080 4241177; www.covodeisaraceni.com.* Very civilised, comfortable hotel with classic-style lobby and breakfast room, different styles of bedroom (including contemporary suites) and a wonderful setting on the cliffs. The restaurant is set on three sea-view terraces, one of which only opens in summer.

Masseria della Zingara €€€€ *Contrada Selva Fina 1000, Polignano a Mare; for bookings and enquiries contact Andrew Salmon on 0044 (0)7967 687642; www.masseriadellazingara.com.* Set among eight hectares (20 acres) of olive, cherry and almond groves, 7km (4.5 miles) inland from Polignano, this is an early 18th-century *masseria*, lovingly restored by its British owners. The emphasis is on switching off, and there are specialist courses in yoga and textiles. The atmosphere is more 'house party' than 'hotel' and it is ideal for private rental (minimum one week) either for family groups or large parties of friends.

Savelletri di Fasano

Borgo Egnazia €€€€ *Strada Comunale Egnazia, Savelletri di Fasano; tel: 080 2255850; https://borgoegnazia.com.* The Borgo styles itself a 'Nowhere Else Place' and there is certainly nowhere else like it in Puglia. It is a high-end resort, dedicated to pure luxury and attracting celebrities (Justin Timberlake married Jessica Biel here) and wealthy European families. Designed on the lines of a Puglian village (though built from scratch) it comprises low-rise, sun-bleached buildings including villas with private pools, and offers every conceivable facility including a Michelin-starred restaurant, a unique spa (see page 91), championship golf course and two private beaches.

Masseria Cimino €€€€ *Contrada Masciola, Savelletri di Fasano; tel: 080 4827886;* www.masseriacimino.com. This tranquil and exclusive getaway is close to the sea and bordering the Roman remains of Egnazia. It is a family-run, relatively small and intimate *masseria*, with 14 whitewashed rooms in the old farmhouse and ancient tower. Most guests book half board and enjoy delicious buffet-style dinners with vegetables straight from the kitchen garden. Golfers can take advantage of the nearby San Domenico golf course.

Masseria San Domenico €€€€ *Strada Provinciale 90, Savelletri di Fasano; tel: 080 4827769;* www.masseriasandomenico.com. One of the first *masseria* conversions and now part of the Leading Hotels of the World group, the five-star San Domenico lies 500 metres/yards from the Adriatic coast, among ancient olive groves. The resort is the height of luxury (which you might expect from the prices), boasting a state-of-the art wellness and thalassotherapy centre, 18-hole golf course, huge sea-water swimming pool and a private beach club with a superb fish restaurant. The *masseria* produces its own vegetables, fruit and olive oil. It is peaceful and relaxing, with gracious and discreet service. No children.

Masseria Torre Coccaro €€€€ *Contrada Coccaro, 8, Savelletri di Fasano; tel: 080 4829310;* www.masseriatorrecoccaro.com. Arguably the loveliest of the *masserie* in the region, offering traditional charm, sea views, elegant rooms and suites and first-class food. A shuttle bus quickly links it to the region's plushest beach club, the Coccaro, with a long sandy beach, private gazebos, massage opportunities under the palms and seafood and cocktails served at your sunbed.

Selva di Fasano

Tenuta Monacelle €€€ *Strada Monacelle, Selva di Fasano; tel: 080 9309942;* www.tenutamonacelle.com. Secluded amid 20 hectares (50 acres) of farmland and cherry trees, 16km (10 miles) south of Monopoli, this is a *trulli* village where guests can opt to stay in one of the seven quaint conical *trulli* or the more comfortable accommodation (with AC and TV) in newer buildings dotted around the complex. A free shuttle service links the hotel with the two nearby beaches (20 mins) or you can relax by the lovely pool in the gardens. Local Puglian specialities are served in Il Ciliegeto, the hotel restaurant.

PUGLIA IMPERIALE

Trani

Palazzo Filisio Hotel €€€ *Via Mons. Addazi 2, Trani; tel: 0883 500931.* You can't get more central than this charming four-star hotel in the shadow of Trani's famous cathedral by the sea. It is a small hotel within the elegant 18th-century Palazzo Filisio. Guest rooms are modern and comfortable, many with views of the sea and cathedral. The Regia restaurant is well worth trying for its fish and seafood. Look out for special dinner, bed and breakfast deals.

VALLE D'ITRIA

Locorotondo

Truddhi Casa e Cucina di Puglia €€ *Strada Provinciale 226, Contrada Trito 161, Locorotondo; tel: 340 4130855; www.truddhi.com.* Alberobello, famous for its multitude of *trulli*, has numerous dwellings to rent but the nearby Truddhi complex, close to the lovely town of Locorotondo, offers a more peaceful, rural destination. The *trulli* are set amid vines and olive groves, in the unspoilt Itria Valley, and are run by an Italian and his Welsh wife. Nothing is too much trouble for them. The *trulli* come with kitchenette, and private patios. Guests have the use of a beautiful pool area (open May to September); yoga classes and massage services can be arranged. In high season there is normally a minimum stay of three nights.

Montalbano

Masseria Lamiola Piccola €€ *Contrada Lamiola Piccola, Montalbano; tel: 348 7678370; www.lamiolapiccola.com.* This is a peaceful farmhouse in the heart of the countryside 12km (7.5 miles) from Ostuni and 8km (5 miles) from the Adriatic beaches. It is a delightfully relaxing place to stay, with charming hosts who will help sort out your itinerary and recommend restaurants in the area. There are six guest rooms, all with AC and minibar, simply but charmingly furnished with wrought-iron beds, vaulted ceilings, dark-wood furniture and whitewashed walls.

Ostuni

Masseria Il Frantoio €€€ *SS16 Km 874, Ostuni; tel: 0831 330276;* www.masseriailfrantoio.it. In the countryside, not far from Ostuni, this appealing and popular farmhouse is one of the original *masserie*. Here you can indulge in the eight, six or four-course organic lunches or dinners, feasting at communal tables on the finest of the region's cuisine, with fresh ingredients and fabulous olive oil from the farm. Luciano will explain each course and make sure the glasses are kept full. The 16 character guest rooms have rustic and antique furnishings and white tiled bathrooms. An inviting swimming pool is set in the olive grove and the sea is only 5km (3 miles) away.

SALENTO
Corigliano d'Otranto

Masseria Sant'Angelo Agriturismo € *Case Sparse Sant'Angelo, Corigliano d'Otranto; tel: 0836 320575;* www.masseriasantangelo.it. This an authentic, family-run working farm, with organically grown produce and simple guest rooms. Think goats, horses and hens rather than TVs and air-conditioning. The hosts are delightful and hugely helpful. Delicious dinners are served around three times a week, occasionally featuring a demonstration of Pizzica, a traditional form of music and dance.

Lecce

Centro Storico B&B € *Via Andrea Vignes, 2, Lecce; tel: 083 2242 727;* www.centrostoricolecce.it. Charming B&B in the historic Palazzo Astore, a short walk from the main monuments of Lecce. A panoramic terrace, with hammocks, hot tub and massage tables, overlooks rooftops and church towers.

Rooms have tea and coffee-making facilities but for breakfast you are given a voucher for a nearby café. The best room is the Duomo Suite which can be found at the top with its own private terrace, but do note that the B&B has no lift available.

Risorgimento Resort €€–€€€ *Via Augusto Imperatore 19, Lecce; tel: 0832 246311;* www.risorgimentoresort.com. Housed in an early 19th-century *palazzo* in a conveniently central but not-too-noisy street, the Risorgimento was once a famous meeting-place of politicians. Today it is a contemporary hotel with 47 rooms and suites, fitness centre, gourmet cuisine and, in summer, a rooftop bar/restaurant. For a five-star hotel prices are very reasonable.

Santa Chiara €–€€; *Via degli Ammirati, Lecce; 24; tel: 0832 304998;* www.santachiaralecce.it. Charming boutique hotel within an elegant *palazzo* in the heart of the city. The 21 guest rooms come in various categories, according to view and size, but all are furnished in traditional style, with neutral colours. Rates are very reasonable for a four-star hotel but cheapest rooms are on the small side, and it can get quite noisy. A buffet breakfast is served on the roof garden during the summer, which also has a lively bar for you to enjoy a drink or two.

Otranto

Masseria Panareo €€ *Parco di Porto Badisco, Otranto; tel: 0836 812 999;.* www.masseriapanareo.com. Beautifully renovated *masseria* with lovely pool and location. Guest rooms vary according to price, but all are light, tastefully furnished and perfectly comfortable. The new rooms have their own private courtyard. The hotel is known for its cuisine, and meals can be enjoyed on the veranda with fine views of the coast and surrounding countryside. It is a short taxi ride (or you can enjoy a bike ride) to the lovely, secluded bay of Porto Badisco.

Palazzo de Mori €€ *Bastione dei Pelasgi, Otranto; tel: 0836 801 088.* In the historical centre this B&B has ten whitewashed rooms overlooking the port, sea or castle. Breakfast (continental with home-made cakes) or drinks can be taken on the charming roof terrace.

Ugento

Castello di Ugento €€€€ *Via Castello 13, Ugento; tel: 0833 1850 720;* www.castellodiugento.com. No expense was spared in the restoration of this 17th-century castle and in its conversion into a five-star boutique hotel and cookery school. It retains 17th-century frescoes and has contemporary art exhibition space on the first floor. The nine deluxe rooms and suites combine period features with sleek contemporary Italian design. Cuisine is superb, with produce from the 18th-century kitchen garden. The coast is 7km (4 miles) away. There is no swimming pool but guests can use the facilities of the sister hotel, *Masseria Le Mandorle*, which is only around a5 minutes' drive away.

BASILICATA

Matera

Corte San Pietro €€–€€€ *Via Bruno Buozzi, 97b, Matera; tel: 0835 310813;* www.cortesanpietro.it. A welcoming little hotel in the fascinating Sassi (ancient cave dwellings) of Matera, amid cave churches, alleys and grottoes. The dozen guest rooms are cleverly converted caves in rustic style, though with their contemporary bathrooms, comfy beds, wi-fi and in-room massage, they are a far cry from the former peasant dwellings. Staff are exceptionally helpful – it's almost like staying with friends. Good buffet breakfasts are served in the courtyard in summer.

L'Hotel in Pietra €–€€€ *Via San Giovanni Vecchio 22; tel: 0835 344 040;* www.hotelinpietra.it. Fabulous boutique hotel converted from a 13th-century rupestrian church and perched in the Sasso Barisano. It has peaceful rooms and suites, from small to spacious, and pale stone walls. Staff are really helpful and go out of their way to help plan your itinerary. Some of the deluxe rooms have great views of the Sassi and the cathedral.

Italia €€ *Via Ridola 5, tel: 0835 333 561, www.albergoitalia.com.* Matera Piano's most convenient hotel, where Mel Gibson and his cast stayed, and the best option if you don't fancy sleeping in a cave. Transfers to and from Bari and Ferrandina can be arranged.

INDEX

A
Abbazia di Santa Maria di Cerrate 67
accommodation 118
airports 119
Alberobello 53
    Rione Aia Piccola 54
    Rione Monti 53
    Trullo Sovrano 54
Andria 38

B
Bari 46
    Bari Vecchia 47
    Basilica di San Nicola 48
    Castello Normanno Svevo 47
    Cattedrale di San Sabino 47
    Chiesa di San Gregorio 48
    Museo del Succorpo della Cattedrale 48
    Piazza Mercantile 49
Barletta 39
Brindisi 61
    Duomo 62
    Monumento Al Marinaio d'Italia 61
    Museo Archeologico Provinciale Ribezzo 62
    Palazzo Granafei-Nervegna 63
    Roman Column 62
    Scalinata Virgiliana 62
    Tempio di San Giovanni al Sepolcro 63
budgeting 120

C
Calimera 69
camping 121
Canne della Battaglia 41
    Antiquarium 41
    Parco Archeologico di Canne della Battaglia 41
Canosa di Puglia 41
Capocollo di Martina Franca 57
car hire 121
Castel del Monte 38
Castro 73
Cattedrale di San Sabino 42
Chiesa del Santo Sepolcro 39
Cisternino 58
climate 122
Colossus 39
Corigliano d'Otranto 69
crime and safety 122

D
driving 123

E
Egnazia 51
electricity 124
embassies and consulates 124
emergencies 124

F
Foggia 36
Fondazione Museo Pino Pascali 51
Foresta Umbra 28
Frederick II 40

G
Galatina 70
Gallipoli 75
    bastions 76
    Castello Angioino 75
    Cattedrale di Sant'Agata 76
    fish market 76
    Frantoio Ipogeo 76
Grotta Bianca 53
Grottaglie 79
Grotte di Castellana 53
guides and tours 125

I
Il Tavoliere 36
Isole Tremiti 33

L
La Grotta Zinzulusa 73
language 126
La Notte della Taranta 70
Lecce 63
    Basilica di San Giovanni Battista 67
    Basilica di Santa Croce 65
    Chiesa di Santa Chiara 66

Duomo 66
Museo Archeologico Faggiano 67
Piazza del Duomo 66
Piazza Sant'Oronzo 64
Roman Amphitheatre 64
Sedile 64
LGBTQ travellers 126
Locorotondo 54
Lucera 36

M

maps 127
Marina di Pescoluse 75
Martina Franca 55
Chiesa di San Martino 57
Palazzo Ducale 56
Piazza Plebiscito 57
Piazza XX Settembre 56
Porto Santo Stefano 56
Matera 80
Casa-Grotta di Vico Solitario 84
Cattedrale di Matera 85
Chiesa di Madonna delle Virtù 83
Chiesa di San Nicola dei Greci 83
Chiesa di Santa Lucia alle Malve 84
Chiesa San Pietro Barisano 83
Chiesa Santa Maria de Idris 83
Palombaro Lungo 85
Parco della Murgia Materana 85
Piazza Vittorio Veneto 85
San Giovanni in Monterrone 83
Sasso Barisano 83
Sasso Caveoso 83
media 127
money 127
Monopoli 51
Monte Sant'Angelo 28
Baia delle Zagare 30
Norman castle 29
Santuario di San Michele 28
Tomba di Rotari 29

O

opening hours 128
Ostuni 59
Cattedrale 60
Chiesa di San Francesco 59
Museo di Civiltà Preclassiche della Murgia Meridionale 59
Obelisco di Sant'Oronzo 59
Piazza della Libertà 59
Otranto 70
Baia dei Turchi 72
Basilica di San Pietro 72
Capella dei Martiri 71
Castello Aragonese 71
Cattedrale dell'Annunziata 71

P

Padre Pio 33
Peschici 31
Al Vecchio Frantoio 31
Castello di Peschici 32

police 128
Polignano a Mare 49
Porto Badisco 73
public holidays 129
Puglia Imperiale 37

R

religion 129
Rodi Garganico 32

S

sagne n'cannulate 64
San Domino 35
San Nicola 35
Santa Maria di Leuca 73
Basilica Santuario di Santa Maria de Finibus Terrae 74

T

tarantella 79
Taras (Taranto) 77
Cappellone di San Cataldo 79
Castello Aragonese 78
Cattedrale di San Cataldo 79
Chiesa di San Domenico 79
Convento Santa Chiara 78
Doric Columns 78
Museo Archeologico Nazionale (MArTA) 77
Palazzo di Città 78
telephone 130
The Great Apulian Aqueduct 75
time zones 130

INDEX

tipping 131
toilets 131
tourist information 131
trabucchi 31
Trani 42
    Castello Svevo 43
    Cattedrale di San
        Nicola Pellegrino 42
    Chiesa di Ognissanti 45
    Scolagrande 44
    Scolanova 44
    Villa Comunale 45
transport 132
travellers with disabilities 133
Troia 36
trulli 54

V

Valle d'Itria 52

Vieste 30
    Spiaggia di Pizzomunno 31
    Spiaggia di Scialmarino 31

W

websites and internet access 134

THE MINI ROUGH GUIDE TO
PUGLIA

First Edition 2022

Editor: Zara Sekhavati
Author: Susie Boulton
Picture Editor: Tom Smyth
Cartography Update: Carte
Layout: Pradeep Thapliyal
Head of DTP and Pre-Press: Katie Bennett
Head of Publishing: Kate Drynan
Photography Credits: Getty Images 16, 19, 21, 22, 23, 101, 102, 105; iStock 4MC, 4ML, 5T, 5M, 5M, 6B, 12, 29, 34, 38, 49, 50, 55, 58, 60, 66, 82; Leonardo 90; Shutterstock 1, 4TC, 4TC, 4TL, 6T, 7T, 7B, 11, 17, 24, 26, 30, 32, 35, 37, 41, 43, 44, 45, 46, 52, 56, 61, 62, 65, 68, 70, 72, 74, 76, 78, 80, 83, 93, 96, 106, 108; © ARET Pugliapromozione/Andrea Ruggeri 92; © ARET Pugliapromozione/Franco Cappellari 4ML; © ARET Pugliapromozione/Helmut Berta 86; © ARET Pugliapromozione/Kash Gabriele Torsello 98; © ARET Pugliapromozione/Vanda Biffani 89; © ARET Pugliapromozione/Vittorio Giannella 4MC
Cover Credits: Alberobello trulli Stefano Valeri/Shutterstock

Distribution

UK, Ireland and Europe: Apa Publications (UK) Ltd; sales@roughguides.com
United States and Canada: Ingram Publisher Services; ips@ingramcontent.com
Australia and New Zealand: Booktopia; retailer@booktopia.com.au
Worldwide: Apa Publications (UK) Ltd; sales@roughguides.com

Special Sales, Content Licensing and CoPublishing
Rough Guides can be purchased in bulk quantities at discounted prices. We can create special editions, personalised jackets and corporate imprints tailored to your needs. sales@roughguides.com; http://roughguides.com

All Rights Reserved
© 2022 Apa Digital AG
License edition © Apa Publications Ltd UK

This book was produced using **Typefi** automated publishing software.

Printed in China

No part of this book may be reproduced, stored in a retrieval system or transmitted in any form or means electronic, mechanical, photocopying, recording or otherwise, without written permission from Apa Publications.

Contact us
Every effort has been made to provide accurate information in this publication, but changes are inevitable. The publisher cannot be held responsible for any resulting loss, inconvenience or injury sustained by any traveller as a result of information or advice contained in the guide. We would appreciate it if readers would call our attention to any errors or outdated information, or if you feel we've left something out. Please send your comments with the subject line "Rough Guide Mini Puglia Update" to mail@uk.roughguides.com.